## Praise for *Writers On the Edge*

"This book presents a fresh and provoking examination, written across multiple genres like poetry and memoir, of writers and their relationships to drugs, alcohol, and gambling. ...this collection's piercing honesty will captivate and inspire readers. Recommended."
Bracha Goykadosh, *Library Journal*

"All addictions, at bottom, are the same; and each of us who battles addiction is different. I dove into *Writers On The Edge*. When I came up for air, I knew that I was in good company." Mary Sojourner, author
*She Bets Her Life: a true story of gambling addiction*

"An honest, unflinching book about addiction from a tough group of talented writers. These hard-hitters know whereof they speak, and the language in which they speak can be shocking to the uninitiated—naked prose and poetry about potentially fatal cravings the flesh is heir to—drugs, booze, cutting, overeating, depression, suicide. Not everybody makes it through. *Writers On The Edge* is about dependency, and the toll it takes, on the guilty and the innocent alike." Dirk Hanson, author
*The Chemical Carousel*

"Each author in *Writers on the Edge* passionately and emotionally wrote their true story. There is heartbreak, honesty, and courage in every written piece. I recommend it to all writers & readers."
Billy Burgess, *ReviewTheBook.com*

"Recovery from addiction is, at its core, a deeply personal experience rooted in shared pain and hope among those seeking freedom from their addictive behaviors. *Writers On The Edge* offers intimate storytelling of such eloquence and insight that readers will be left with genuine insight into the power and complexity of this destructive but fascinating human condition. This book is a must-read for anyone wanting the real-life inside scoop on the human side of what addiction is all about."

Arnold M. Washton, Ph.D., Addiction Psychologist, author, *Treating Alcohol and Drug Problems in Psychotherapy Practice: Doing What Works*

"With unflinching honesty and courage these narratives and poems ultimately shine light into some very dark and ominous corners. I'm sure the anthology was not accidentally subtitled with the word 'speak' as in *22 Writers Speak About Addiction and Dependency*. ...Raab and Brown have assembled a host of accomplished writers and thinkers allowing them to finally give 'voice,' on the page, to their unique stories of healing and survival."

Kathleen Gerard, author of *In Transit*

"I felt so much bravery for these 22 writers opening up their souls to share their tales. I was actually impressed to see a few stories regarding food addiction, something I have dealt with in my life. Just like drugs and alcohol, no one is 100% fully recovered because every day life is a trigger and relapse can happen at a moment's notice. The stories both inspired me and gave me hope."

Chrystal Mahan, *SelfEmployedWriter.com*

# Writers On The Edge:

22 Writers Speak About Addiction and Dependency

*Edited by* Diana M. Raab and James Brown

Foreword by Jerry Stahl

Reflections of America Series

MODERN HISTORY PRESS

Writers On The Edge: 22 Writers Speak About Addiction and Dependency
Copyright (c) 2012 by Diana M. Raab and James Brown.
All Rights Reserved.
2nd Printing November 2012

From the Reflections of America Series

*For a complete list of work which has been reprinted in this volume please consult Acknowledgments beginning on p. 167.*

Library of Congress Cataloging-in-Publication Data
Writers on the edge : 22 writers speak about addiction and dependency / edited by Diana M. Raab and James Brown ; foreword by Jerry Stahl.
    p. cm. -- (Reflections of America)
  Includes index.
   ISBN 978-1-61599-108-2 (pbk. : alk. paper) -- ISBN 978-1-61599-109-9 (hardcover : alk. paper)
  1. Authors, American--21st century--Biography. 2. Addicts--United States--Biography. 3. Addicts--Literary collections. I. Raab, Diana, 1954- II. Brown, James, 1957-
  PS509.A27W74 2012
  810.9'3556--dc23
                                        2011036025

Modern History Press, an imprint of
Loving Healing Press
5145 Pontiac Trail
Ann Arbor, MI 48105

www.ModernHistoryPress.com
Tollfree USA/CAN: 888-761-6268
London, UK: 44-20-331-81304

Distributed by Ingram Book Group (USA/CAN), Bertram's Books (UK/EU)

# CONTENTS

Creative work can act not only as a means of escape from pain, but also as a way of structuring chaotic emotions and thoughts, numbing pain through abstraction and the rigors of disciplined thought, and creating a distance from the source of despair.

~ Kay Redfield Jamison
Author of *Touched with Fire*

# FOREWORD

I really hate the term "edge". Forget the fact that the term, itself, has become a soiled staple of Hollywood producer-speak, with studio execs forever dispatching their legion of hacks to "give them something edgy." Or that it's all but impossible to find advertising copy that doesn't march the word out by way of lending whatever thriller or airport novel or toothpaste the suits are pimping that season some frisson of danger, of savagery, of, God save us all, cred. ("Squeeze a little Squirm on your toothbrush—and you'll have edgy breath all day!") Of late "extreme" may have edged out edge, but the term is still dragged out by those who make their fortunes hustling the public into thinking theirs is a product generated not by corporate jim-jims who want to separate you from your money by conning you into thinking whatever you're buying will transform you from a dweeb to a badass, but by, you know, really edgy people, who've done edgy things, in an edgy way, and if you buy this sweater, pick-up truck, CD, or deodorant, you too will be touched by the sexy, seen-it-all-splendor that separates the be's from the wannabe's.

The truth, of course, is that anyone who tells you they're living on the edge is, almost by definition, deluding themselves—or trying to delude you—in the same way that guys who talk tough generally aren't. Because the ones who are, will never say anything about it. They don't have to. What's more, as anyone will tell you who's actually lived there, the edge is not on the edge at all. It's in the middle. Select any story or poem from the collection you have in your twitching little fingers right now, and you will see.

Whether you were a drunk or a cutter, a gambler or overeater or dope fiend, the dirty little secret is that whatever
habit you ultimately have to quit to continue living does not
exist on the periphery of your existence. It exists in the
middle. Everything else is just what you do until you do the
thing you can't stop thinking about doing. Your life
revolves around the drink or the drug or the fuck or the cut
or the bet or whatever the addiction happens to be.

The dirty little secret of our confessional era is that
anyone who has, to employ yet another cliché, "been there
and back" now believes they have the right, if not the
money-making opportunity and duty, to write a memoir (or
a mini-series, or a concept album, or a trilogy in verse)
about their experience. Just as we, happily, have the right
not to read or watch or listen to it.

Which—wasn't that an edgy way to start a book about
life "on the edge?"—brings us to the good news. Simply
put, I don't trust anyone who hasn't been to hell. I can be
friendly, respectful, kind, but those who don't, have that
look in their eye. The no-need-for-words thing that lets one
survivor know they are in the presence of another. And, to a
man and woman, everyone in this extraordinary volume
has, at one time or another, not just gotten their mail in
hell, but even more "intense" (we can't forget about
"intense!") they have not known, for certain, whether they
were ever going to make it out. Not, I hasten to add,
because they were "victims". (And nobody, as the great
Hubert Selby used to say, can clear a room like a victim.)
Quite the opposite. These writers were more often than not,
perps—their own or somebody else's. It's roughly akin to
reading a recollection of Nagasaki survivors by people who
dropped the bomb on themselves.

America, at this point in time, may not manufacture
much. But we do manufacture addicts. According to some
statistics, one out of four citizens in this fine nation qualifies
for that grim and perplexing title. (And no doubt their
family, friends, co-workers, cell-mates, bed-partners, bar

dawgs and drug buddies have the scars to prove it.) But fuck statistics. What the tremendously brave, eloquent, and (occasionally) hysterical writers in this volume offer are the kind of stories that only veterans can tell. I speak for the record, as one who has done some personal research of his own on the subject of addiction. Not that a decade and change on the needle gives you an expert's badge. What it does give you, along with the usual liver damage and lifetime of amends, is an incredible nose for bullshit. Plus an appreciation—make that reverence—for the truth. And the redemptive powers only the truth can unleash.

Open to any piece in this collection, and the scalding, unflinching, overwhelming truths within will shine light on places most people never look. Because they never have to. As addicts, however, we have no choice.

Anyone who reads this book, be they users or used, will put it down changed. And when they raise their eyes from the very last page, the world they see may be redeemed, as well.

~ Jerry Stahl
Author of *Permanent Midnight*

# PREFACE

Use the word *addiction* and the first images that come to mind are ones of pills, powders, needles, crack pipes, and bottles of booze. Most of us might picture a homeless man staggering down the street clutching a brown paper bag in one hand, or a bone-thin junkie with a syringe dangling from his arm.

But times have changed.

Minus the severe physical, potentially life-threatening withdrawal symptoms of the alcoholic or narcotics addict, today's definition of addiction includes all kinds of compulsive behavior. Gambling. Sex. Overeating. Even love. Chronic depression and suicide also fit neatly into the subject, for it is hard, if not unwise, to separate them from the conversation, given that as often as not they most certainly feed into the same tributary.

*Writers On The Edge* challenges the traditional boundaries of the term addiction to include the two most basic elements that define it: obsession and the compulsion to self-destruct. And what distinguishes this book from so many others on the subject is that it is written by well-published writers and poets who have been *there*, on the edge, who know the hellish terrain of addiction, obsession and mental illness, and through their art take us to those dark places with them. Some discover light at the end of the tunnel. Others do not.

The causes of addiction have been identified as genetic, physical and spiritual. Addiction, for many, is the result of an attempt to cover up psychic, emotional or physical pain, and in some cases reflects an unconscious and non-violent form of suicide. According to psychologist Stanislav Grof, the deepest force behind alcoholism and addiction is an unrecognized and perhaps misguided craving for transcendence. Thus, it could be thought that the writers in this collection are searching for something beyond what readily meets the eye. As complicated as the subject may seem, the message is simple. There are those who by whatever means necessary will turn their lives around and survive as a result, and others whose obsessions will consume them. Those chosen for this anthology skillfully articulate their personal struggles, triumphs, and failures, presenting poignant perspectives for reflection, concern and acknowledgement of addiction and its associated issues.

In Scott Russell Sanders' classic essay, "Under the Influence", we witness the slow, painful disintegration of Sanders' alcoholic father. It is a story of a father and son, and their unrealized love, stunted if not destroyed by alcoholism.

For Chase Twichell's "Toys in the Attic", the journey takes us deep into the psyche of the chronically depressed, having lived for fifteen years "with psychoactive drugs in my brain, among them Ambien, Celexa, Desyrel, Effexor, Elavil, Pamelor, Paxil, Serzone, Traivil, Valium, Wellbutrin, and Xanax." The goal is to stabilize mood rather than heighten or distort it as one does with alcohol and narcotics. But how do these psychotropic drugs affect consciousness? And how, in turn, does a consciousness altered by these drugs influence Twichell's poetry, which she describes as "the ultimate art of self-annihilation"?

Add to the mix "Pretty Red Stripes" by Linda Gray Sexton (daughter of the late poet Anne Sexton, who committed suicide), and you have a stunningly graphic account of that obsessive, destructive practice known as "cutting". Like a drug, drawing a razor through one's skin brings to some, a sense of relief, pleasure, and release. "It's a way of letting the poison out," Sexton writes, "To bleed is a way of knowing you're alive."

That same need for "knowing you're alive" segues smoothly into Sue William Silverman's book excerpt, "Last Day Out," on sex addiction. The need, the compulsion, the obsession for a heightened sense of pleasure once again crosses the line between what society considers normal versus abnormal behavior. Here is a woman who feels marriage a mundane institution in which she can never be content, and so feels compelled to regularly engage in one night stands with strange men for what she refers to as a need to be "loved".

In "The Doppler Effect", renowned poet B.H. Fairchild masterfully captures the essence of the unspoken sadness and self-alienation drinkers feel simply sitting in a darkened bar, wondering *why* they are there, and if not realizing, at least coming to suppose that *belonging* of any sort is at best perhaps an illusion.

We join and honor the other fine writers and poets in this collection, including, John Amen, Frederick and Steven Barthelme, Kera Bolonik, Maud Casey, Anna David, Denise Duhamel, Ruth Fowler, David Huddle, Margaret Bullitt-Jonas, Gregory Orr, Victoria Patterson, Molly Peacock, Perie Longo, Stephen Jay Schwartz, and Rachel Yoder. They all follow in the great, though unfortunate tradition of their literary predecessors. Charles Baudelaire. Edgar Allen Poe. Jack London. Ernest Hemingway. F. Scott Fitzgerald. William Styron. Dorothy Parker. Virginia Wolff. Raymond Carver. Tennessee Williams. Eugene O'Neil. Jean Rhys. Truman Capote. The list of alcoholic, drug addicted, suicidal, chronically depressed and mentally ill writers goes on and on. But don't be misled. Though some might consider these afflictions simply an occupational hazard of being an artist, for each name here there are dozens of others who have lived healthy, clean and sober lives and produced great works.

It is hoped that this anthology will be helpful to all artistic personalities who wish to gain a stronger sense of how their colleagues navigate their way through addiction, mental illness, suicide, and other obsessive, self-destructive behaviors. These battles are not fought alone and perhaps these stories will also provide insight and hope to all those and their loved ones struggling with some form of addiction and its inevitable consequences.

~ Diana M. Raab and James Brown,
Editors

# WRITING FOR LIFE

## Perie Longo

On the edge
he signs his name
with a skid mark
voice a hollow drum
willow without stretch of deer skin
to bring the rain.

Having been on the edge ourselves,
the long way down—or up—
either way barely bearable
we hide behind neatly dressed words.

He writes in such a jumble
(word salad
with blood dressing)

no one understands but that's the whole idea.

Last time someone figured it out
he was sent down the river
(figure of speech) to get his head screwed on
straight
straight
straight

locked in a room
full of curve balls.

"I just wanted to stand out," he says
slinging up the umbrella of his misfortune.
"As if your nails are trying to hang
onto the sky?" I ask (up talk it's called).

He laughs a cry,
his strong hand over his wet, pale cheek.
Curse the screw of chemicals
that leave who we love tweaked
and double crossed.

# UNDER THE INFLUENCE

## Scott Russell Sanders

My father drank. He drank as a gut-punched boxer gasps for breath, as a starving dog gobbles food—compulsively, secretly, in pain and trembling. I use the past tense not because he ever quit drinking but because he quit living. That is how the story ends for my father, age sixty-four, heart bursting, body cooling and forsaken on the linoleum of my brother's trailer. The story continues for my brother, my sister, my mother, and me, and it will continue so long as memory holds.

In the perennial present of memory, I slip into the garage or barn to see my father tipping back the flat green bottles of wine, the brown cylinders of whiskey, the cans of beer disguised in paper bags. His Adam's apple bobs, the liquid gurgles, he wipes the sandy-haired back of a hand over his lips, and then, his bloodshot gaze bumping into me, he stashes the bottle or can inside his jacket, under the workbench, between two bales of hay, and we both pretend the moment has not occurred.

"What's up, buddy?" he says, thick-tongued and edgy.

"Sky's up," I answer, playing along.

"And don't forget prices," he grumbles. "Prices are always up. And taxes."

In memory, his white 1951 Pontiac with the stripes down the hood and the Indian head on the snout jounces to a stop in the driveway; or it is the 1956 Ford station wagon, or the 1963 Rambler shaped like a toad, or the sleek 1969 Bonneville that will do 120 miles per hour on straightaways; or it is the robin's-egg blue pickup, new in 1980, battered in 1981, the year of his death. He climbs out, grinning dangerously, unsteady on his legs, and we children interrupt our game of catch, our building of snow forts, our picking of plums, to watch in silence as he weaves past into the house, where he slumps into his overstuffed chair and falls asleep. Shaking her head, our mother stubs out the cigarette he has left smoldering in the ashtray. All evening, until our bedtimes, we tiptoe past him, as past a snoring dragon. Then we curl in our fearful sheets, listening. Eventually he wakes with a grunt, Mother slings accusations at him, he snarls back, she yells, he growls, their voices clashing. Before long, she retreats to their bedroom, sobbing—not from the blows of fists, for he never strikes her, but from the force of words.

Left alone, our father prowls the house, thumping into furniture, rummaging in the kitchen, slamming doors, turning the pages of the newspaper with a savage crackle, muttering back at the late-night drivel from television. The roof might fly off, the walls might buckle from the pressure of his rage. Whatever my brother and sister and mother may be thinking on their own rumpled pillows, I lie there hating him, loving him, fearing him, knowing I have failed him. I tell myself he drinks to ease an ache that gnaws at his belly, an ache I must have caused by disappointing him somehow, a murderous ache I should be able to relieve by doing all my chores, earning A's in school, winning baseball games, fixing the broken washer and the burst pipes, bringing in money to fill his empty wallet. He would not hide the green bottles in his tool box, would not sneak off to the barn with a lump under his coat, would not fall asleep in the daylight, would not roar and fume, would not drink himself to death, if only I were perfect.

I am forty-two as I write these words, and I know full well that my father was an alcoholic, a man consumed by disease rather than by disappointment. What had seemed to me a private grief is in fact a public scourge. In the United

States alone, some ten or fifteen million people share his ailment, and behind the doors they slam in fury or disgrace, countless other children tremble. I comfort myself with such knowledge, holding it against the throb of memory like an ice pack against a bruise. There are keener sources of grief: poverty, racism, rape, war. I do not wish to compete for a trophy in suffering. I am only trying to understand the corrosive mixture of helplessness, responsibility, and shame that I learned to feel as the son of an alcoholic. I realize now that I did not cause my father's illness, nor could I have cured it. Yet for all this grown-up knowledge, I am still ten years old, my own son's age, and as that boy I struggle in guilt and confusion to save my father from pain.

* * *

Consider a few of our synonyms for *drunk*: tipsy, tight, pickled, soused, and plowed; stoned and stewed, lubricated and inebriated, juiced and sluiced; three sheets to the wind, in your cups, out of your mind, under the table; lit up, tanked up, wiped out; besotted, blotto, bombed, and buzzed; plastered, polluted, putrefied; loaded or looped, boozy, woozy, fuddled, or smashed; crocked and shit-faced, corked and pissed, snockered and sloshed.

It is a mostly humorous lexicon, as the lore that deals with drunks—in jokes and cartoons, in plays, films, and television skits—is largely comic. Aunt Matilda nips elderberry wine from the sideboard and burps politely during supper. Uncle Fred slouches to the table glassy-eyed, wearing a lampshade for a hat and murmuring, "Candy is dandy but liquor is quicker." Inspired by cocktails, Mrs. Somebody recounts the events of her day in a fuzzy dialect, while Mr. Somebody nibbles her ear and croons a bawdy song. On the sofa with Boyfriend, Daughter giggles, licking gin from her lips, and loosens the bows in her hair. Junior knocks back some brews with his chums at the Leopard Lounge and stumbles home to the wrong house, wonders foggily why he cannot locate his pajamas, and crawls naked into bed with the ugliest girl in school. The family dog slurps from a neglected martini and wobbles to the nursery, where he vomits in Baby's shoe.

It is all great fun. But if in the audience you notice a few laughing faces turn grim when the drunk lurches on stage, don't be surprised, for these are the children of alcoholics. Over the grinning mask of Dionysus, the leering mask of Bacchus, these children cannot help seeing the bloated features of their own parents. Instead of laughing, they wince, they mourn. Instead of celebrating the drunk as one freed from constraints, they pity him as one enslaved. They refuse to believe *in vino veritas*, having seen their befuddled parents skid away from truth toward folly and oblivion. And so these children bite their lips until the lush staggers into the wings.

My father, when drunk, was neither funny nor honest; he was pathetic, frightening, deceitful. There seemed to be a leak in him somewhere, and he poured in booze to keep from draining dry. Like a torture victim who refuses to squeal, he would never admit that he had touched a drop, not even in his last year, when he seemed to be dissolving in alcohol before our very eyes. I never knew him to lie about anything, ever, except about this one ruinous fact. Drowsy, clumsy, unable to fix a bicycle tire, throw a baseball, balance a grocery sack, or walk across the room, he was stripped of his true self by drink. In a matter of minutes, the contents of a bottle could transform a brave man into a coward, a buddy into a bully, a gifted athlete and skilled carpenter and shrewd businessman into a bumbler. No dictionary of synonyms for *drunk* would soften the anguish of watching our prince turn into a frog.

\* \* \*

Father's drinking became the family secret. While growing up, we children never breathed a word of it beyond the four walls of our house. To this day, my brother and sister rarely mention it, and then only when I press them. I did not confess the ugly, bewildering fact to my wife until his wavering walk and slurred speech forced me to. Recently, on the seventh anniversary of my father's death, I asked my mother if she ever spoke of his drinking to friends. "No, no, never," she replied hastily. "I couldn't bear for anyone to know."

The secret bores under the skin, gets in the blood, into the bone, and stays there. Long after you have supposedly been cured of malaria, the fever can flare up, the tremors can shake you. So it is with the fevers of shame. You swallow the bitter quinine of knowledge, and you learn to feel pity and compassion toward the drinker. Yet the shame lingers in your marrow, and, because of the shame, anger.

\* \* \*

For a long stretch of my childhood we lived on a military reservation in Ohio, an arsenal where bombs were stored underground in bunkers and vintage airplanes burst into flames and unstable artillery shells boomed nightly at the dump. We had the feeling, as children, that we played in a minefield, where a heedless footfall could trigger an explosion. When Father was drinking, the house, too, became a minefield. The least bump could set off either parent.

The more he drank, the more obsessed Mother became with stopping him. She hunted for bottles, counted the cash in his wallet, sniffed at his breath. Without meaning to snoop, we children blundered left and right into damning evidence. On afternoons when he came home from work sober, we flung ourselves at him for hugs, and felt against our ribs the telltale lump in his coat. In the barn we tumbled on the hay and heard beneath our sneakers the crunch of buried glass. We tugged open a drawer in his workbench, looking for screwdrivers or crescent wrenches, and spied a gleaming six-pack among the tools. Playing tag, we darted around the house just in time to see him sway on the rear stoop and heave a finished bottle into the woods. In his good night kiss we smelled the cloying sweetness of Clorets, the mints he chewed to camouflage his dragon's breath.

I can summon up that kiss right now by recalling Theodore Roethke's lines about his own father:

*The whiskey on your breath*
*Could make a small boy dizzy;*
*But I hung on like death:*
*Such waltzing was not easy.*

Such waltzing was hard, terribly hard, for with a boy's scrawny arms I was trying to hold my tipsy father upright.

For years, the chief source of those incriminating bottles and cans was a grimy store a mile from us, a cinder block place called Sly's, with two gas pumps outside and a moth-eaten dog asleep in the window. A strip of flypaper, speckled the year round with black bodies, coiled in the doorway. Inside, on rusty metal shelves or in wheezing coolers, you could find pop and Popsicles, cigarettes, potato chips, canned soup, raunchy postcards, fishing gear, Twinkies, wine, and beer. When Father drove anywhere on errands, Mother would send us kids along as guards, warning us not to let him out of our sight. And so with one or more of us on board, Father would cruise up to Sly's, pump a dollar's worth of gas or plump the tires with air, and then, telling us to wait in the car, he would head for that fly-spangled doorway.

Dutiful and panicky, we cried, "Let us go in with you!"

"No," he answered. "I'll be back in two shakes."

"Please!"

"No!" he roared. "Don't you budge, or I'll jerk a knot in your tails!"

So we stayed put, kicking the seats, while he ducked inside. Often, when he had parked the car at a careless angle, we gazed in through the window and saw Mr. Sly fetching down from a shelf behind the cash register two green pints of Gallo wine. Father swigged one of them right there at the counter, stuffed the other in his pocket, and then out he came, a bulge in his coat, a flustered look on his red face.

Because the Mom and Pop who ran the dump were neighbors of ours, living just down the tar-blistered road, I hated them all the more for poisoning my father. I wanted to sneak in their store and smash the bottles and set fire to the place. I also hated the Gallo brothers, Ernest and Julio, whose jovial faces shone from the labels of their wine, labels I would find, torn and curled, when I burned the trash. I noted the Gallo brothers' address, in California, and I studied the road atlas to see how far that was from Ohio, because I meant to go out there and tell Ernest and Julio what they were doing to my father, and then, if they showed no mercy, I would kill them.

\* \* \*

While growing up on the back roads and in the country schools and cramped Methodist churches of Ohio and Tennessee, I never heard the word *alcoholism*, never happened across it in books or magazines. In the nearby towns, there were no addiction treatment programs, no community mental health centers, no Alcoholics Anonymous chapters, no therapists. Left alone with our grievous secret, we had no way of understanding Father's drinking except as an act of will, a deliberate folly or cruelty, a moral weakness, a sin. He drank because he chose to, pure and simple. Why our father, so playful and competent and kind when sober, would choose to ruin himself and punish his family, we could not fathom.

Our neighborhood was high on the Bible, and the Bible was hard on drunkards. "Woe to those who are heroes at drinking wine, and valiant men in mixing strong drink," wrote Isaiah. "The priest and the prophet reel with strong drink, they are confused with wine, they err in vision, they stumble in giving judgment. For all tables are full of vomit, no place is without filthiness." We children had seen those fouled tables at the local truck stop where the notorious boozers hung out, our father occasionally among them. "Wine and new wine take away the understanding," declared the prophet Hosea. We had also seen evidence of that in our father, who could multiply seven-digit numbers in his head when sober, but when drunk could not help us with fourth-grade math. Proverbs warned: "Do not look at wine when it is red, when it sparkles in the cup and goes down smoothly. At the last it bites like a serpent, and stings like an adder. Your eyes will see strange things, and your mind utter perverse things." Woe, woe.

Dismayingly often, these biblical drunkards stirred up trouble for their own kids. Noah made fresh wine after the flood, drank too much of it, fell asleep without any clothes on, and was glimpsed in the buff by his son Ham, whom Noah promptly cursed. In one passage—it was so shocking we had to read it under our blankets with flashlights—the patriarch Lot fell down drunk and slept with his daughters. The sins of the fathers set their children's teeth on edge.

Our ministers were fond of quoting St. Paul's pronouncement that drunkards would not inherit the kingdom of God. These grave preachers assured us that the wine referred to during the Last Supper was in fact grape juice. Bible and sermons and hymns combined to give us the impression that Moses should have brought down from the mountain another stone tablet, bearing the Eleventh Commandment: Thou shalt not drink.

The scariest and most illuminating Bible story apropos of drunkards was the one about the lunatic and the swine. We knew it by heart: When Jesus climbed out of his boat one day, this lunatic came charging up from the graveyard, stark naked and filthy, frothing at the mouth, so violent that he broke the strongest chains. Nobody would go near him. Night and day for years this madman had been wailing among the tombs and bruising himself with stones. Jesus took one look at him and said, "Come out of the man, you unclean spirits!" for he could see that the lunatic was possessed by demons. Meanwhile, some hogs were conve-

niently rooting nearby. "If we have to come out," begged
the demons, "at least let us go into those swine." Jesus
agreed, the unclean spirits entered the hogs, and the hogs
rushed straight off a cliff and plunged into a lake. Hearing
the story in Sunday school, my friends thought mainly of
the pigs. (How big a splash did they make? Who paid for
the lost pork?) But I thought of the redeemed lunatic, who
bathed himself and put on clothes and calmly sat at the feet
of Jesus, restored—so the Bible said—to "his right mind."

When drunk, our father was clearly in his wrong mind.
He became a stranger, as fearful to us as any graveyard
lunatic, not quite frothing at the mouth but fierce enough,
quick-tempered, explosive; or else he grew maudlin and
weepy, which frightened us nearly as much. In my boyhood
despair, I reasoned that maybe he wasn't to blame for
turning into an ogre: Maybe, like the lunatic, he was
possessed by demons. I found support for my theory when I
heard liquor referred to as "spirits," when the newspapers
reported that somebody had been arrested for "driving
under the influence," and when church ladies railed against
that "demon drink."

If my father was indeed possessed, who would exorcise
him? If he was a sinner, who would save him? If he was ill,
who would cure him? If he suffered, who would ease his
pain? Not ministers or doctors, for we could not bring
ourselves to confide in them; not the neighbors, for we
pretended they had never seen him drunk; not Mother, who
fussed and pleaded but could not budge him; not my
brother and sister, who were only kids. That left me. It did
not matter that I, too, was only a child, and a bewildered
one at that. I could not excuse myself.

* * *

On first reading a description of delirium tremens—in a
book on alcoholism I smuggled from the university
library—I thought immediately of the frothing lunatic and
the frenzied swine. When I read stories or watched films

about grisly metamorphoses—Dr. Jekyll becoming Mr. Hyde, the mild husband changing into a werewolf, the kindly neighbor taken over by a brutal alien—I could not help seeing my own father's mutation from sober to drunk. Even today, knowing better, I am attracted by the demonic theory of drink, for when I recall my father's transformation, the emergence of his ugly second self, I find it easy to believe in possession by unclean spirits. We never knew which version of Father would come home from work, the true or the tainted, nor could we guess how far down the slope toward cruelty he would slide.

How far a man *could* slide we gauged by observing our back-road neighbors—the out-of-work miners who had dragged their families to our corner of Ohio from the desolate hollows of Appalachia, the tightfisted farmers, the surly mechanics, the balked and broken men. There was, for example, whiskey-soaked Mr. Jenkins, who beat his wife and kids so hard we could hear their screams from the road. There was Mr. Lavo the wino, who fell asleep smoking time and again, until one night his disgusted wife bundled up the children and went outside and left him in his easy chair to burn; he awoke on his own, staggered out coughing into the yard, and pounded her flat while the children looked on and the shack turned to ash. There was the truck driver, Mr. Sampson, who tripped over his son's tricycle one night while drunk and got so mad that he jumped into his semi and drove away, shifting through the dozen gears, and never came back. We saw the bruised children of these fathers clump onto our school bus, we saw the abandoned children huddle in the pews at church, we saw the stunned and battered mothers begging for help at our doors.

Our own father never beat us, and I don't think he ever beat Mother, but he threatened often. The Old Testament Yahweh was not more terrible in his wrath. Eyes blazing, voice booming, Father would pull out his belt and swear to give us a whipping, but he never followed through, never needed to, because we could imagine it so vividly. He shoved us, pawed us with the back of his hand, as an irked bear might smack a cub, not to injure, just to clear a space. I can see him grabbing Mother by the hair as she cowers on a chair during a nightly quarrel. He twists her neck back until she gapes up at him, and then he lifts over her skull a glass quart bottle of milk, the milk running down his forearm, and he yells at her, "Say just one more word, one goddamn word, and I'll shut you up!" I fear she will prick him with her sharp tongue, but she is terrified into silence, and so am I, and the leaking bottle quivers in the air, and milk slithers through the red hair of my father's uplifted arm, and the entire scene is there to this moment, the head jerked back, the club raised.

When the drink made him weepy, Father would pack a bag and kiss each of us children on the head, and announce from the front door that he was moving out. "Where to?" we demanded, fearful each time that he would leave for good, as Mr. Sampson had roared away for good in his diesel truck. "Someplace where I won't get hounded every minute," Father would answer, his jaw quivering. He stabbed a look at Mother, who might say, "Don't run into the ditch before you get there," or, "Good riddance," and then he would slink away. Mother watched him go with arms crossed over her chest, her face closed like the lid on a box of snakes. We children bawled. Where could he go? To the truck stop, that den of iniquity? To one of those dark, ratty flophouses in town? Would he wind up sleeping under a railroad bridge or on a park bench or in a cardboard box, mummied in rags, like the bums we had seen on our trips to Cleveland and Chicago? We bawled and bawled, wondering if he would ever come back.

He always did come back, a day or a week later, but each time there was a sliver less of him.

\* \* \*

In Kafka's *Metamorphosis*, which opens famously with Gregor Samsa waking up from uneasy dreams to find himself transformed into an insect, Gregor's family keep reassuring themselves that things will be just fine again, "When he comes back to us." Each time alcohol transformed our father, we held out the same hope, that he would really and truly come back to us, our authentic father, the tender and playful and competent man, and then all things would be fine. We had grounds for such hope. After his weepy departures and chapfallen returns, he would sometimes go weeks, even months, without drinking. Those were glad times. Joy banged inside my ribs. Every day without the furtive glint of bottles, every meal without a fight, every bedtime without sobs encouraged us to believe that such bliss might go on forever.

Mother was fooled by just such a hope all during the forty-odd years she knew this Greeley Ray Sanders. Soon after she met him in a Chicago delicatessen on the eve of World War II, and fell for his butter-melting Mississippi drawl and his wavy red hair, she learned that he drank heavily. But then so did a lot of men. She would soon coax or scold him into breaking the nasty habit. She would point out to him how ugly and foolish it was, this bleary drinking, and then he would quit. He refused to quit during their engagement, however, still refused during the first years of marriage, refused until my sister came along. The shock of fatherhood sobered him, and he remained sober through my birth at the end of the war and right on through until we moved in 1951 to the Ohio arsenal, that paradise of bombs. Like all places that make a business of death, the arsenal had more than its share of alcoholics and drug addicts and other varieties of escape artists. There I turned six and started school and woke into a child's flickering awareness, just in time to see my father begin sneaking swigs in the garage.

He sobered up again for most of a year at the height of the Korean War, to celebrate the birth of my brother. But aside from that dry spell, his only breaks from drinking before I graduated from high school were just long enough to raise and then dash our hopes. Then during the fall of my senior year—the time of the Cuban missile crisis, when it seemed that the nightly explosions at the munitions dump and the nightly rages in our household might spread to engulf the globe—Father collapsed. His liver, kidneys, and heart all conked out. The doctors saved him, but only by a hair. He stayed in the hospital for weeks, going through a withdrawal so terrible that Mother would not let us visit him. If he wanted to kill himself, the doctors solemnly warned him, all he had to do was hit the bottle again. One binge would finish him.

Father must have believed them, for he stayed dry the next fifteen years. It was an answer to prayer, Mother said, it was a miracle. I believe it was a reflex of fear, which he sustained over the years through courage and pride. He knew a man could die from drink, for his brother Roscoe had. We children never laid eyes on doomed Uncle Roscoe, but in the stories Mother told us he became a fairy tale figure, like a boy who took the wrong turning in the woods and was gobbled up by the wolf.

The fifteen-year dry spell came to an end with Father's retirement in the spring of 1978. Like many men, he gave up his identity along with his job. One day he was a boss at the factory, with a brass plate on his door and a reputation to uphold; the next day he was a nobody at home. He and Mother were leaving Ontario, the last of the many places to which his job had carried them, and they were moving to a new house in Mississippi, his childhood stomping grounds. As a boy in Mississippi, Father sold Coca-Cola during dances while the moonshiners peddled their brew in the parking lot; as a young blade, he fought in bars and in the ring, winning a state Golden Gloves championship; he gambled at poker, hunted pheasants, raced motorcycles and cars, played semi-professional baseball, and, along with all his buddies—in the Black Cat Saloon, behind the cotton gin, in the woods—he drank. It was a perilous youth to dream of recovering.

After his final day of work, Mother drove on ahead with a car full of begonias and violets, while Father stayed behind to oversee the packing. When the van was loaded, the sweaty movers broke open a six-pack and offered him a beer.

"Let's drink to retirement!" they crowed. "Let's drink to freedom! to fishing! hunting! loafing! Let's drink to a guy who's going home!"

At least I imagine some such words, for that is all I can do, imagine, and I see Father's hand trembling in midair as he thinks about the fifteen sober years and about the doctors' warning, and he tells himself *Goddamnit, I am a free man, and Why can't a free man drink one beer after a lifetime of hard work?* and I see his arm reaching, his fingers closing, the can tilting to his lips. I even supply a label for the beer, a swaggering brand that promises on television to deliver the essence of life. I watch the amber liquid pour down his throat, the alcohol steal into his blood, the key turn in his brain.

\* \* \*

Soon after my parents moved back to Father's treacherous stomping ground, my wife and I visited them in Mississippi with our five-year-old daughter. Mother had been too distraught to warn me about the return of the demons. So when I climbed out of the car that bright July morning and saw my father napping in the hammock, I felt uneasy, and when he lurched upright and blinked his bloodshot eyes and greeted us in a syrupy voice, I was hurled back helpless into childhood.

"What's the matter with Papaw?" our daughter asked.

"Nothing," I said. "Nothing!"

Like a child again, I pretended not to see him in his stupor, and behind my phony smile I grieved. On that visit and on the few that remained before his death, once again I found bottles in the workbench, bottles in the woods. Again his hands shook too much for him to run a saw, to make his precious miniature furniture, to drive straight down back roads. Again he wound up in the ditch, in the hospital, in jail, in treatment centers. Again he shouted and wept. Again he lied. "I never touched a drop," he swore. "Your mother's making it up."

I no longer fancied I could reason with the men whose names I found on the bottles—Jim Beam, Jack Daniels—nor did I hope to save my father by burning down a store. I was able now to press the cold statistics about alcoholism against the ache of memory: ten million victims, fifteen million, twenty. And yet, in spite of my age, I reacted in the same blind way as I had in childhood, ignoring biology, forgetting numbers, vainly seeking to erase through my efforts whatever drove him to drink. I worked on their place twelve and sixteen hours a day, in the swelter of Mississippi summers, digging ditches, running electrical wires, planting trees, mowing grass, building sheds, as though what nagged at him was some list of chores, as though by taking his worries on my shoulders I could redeem him. I was flung back into boyhood, acting as though my father would not drink himself to death if only I were perfect.

I failed of perfection; he succeeded in dying. To the end, he considered himself not sick but sinful. "Do you want to kill yourself?" I asked him. "Why not?" he answered. "Why the hell not? What's there to save?" To the end, he would not speak about his feelings, would not or could not give a name to the beast that was devouring him.

In silence, he went rushing off the cliff. Unlike the biblical swine, however, he left behind a few of the demons to haunt his children. Life with him and the loss of him twisted us into shapes that will be familiar to other sons and daughters of alcoholics. My brother became a rebel, my sister retreated into shyness, I played the stalwart and dutiful son who would hold the family together. If my father was unstable, I would be a rock. If he squandered money on drink, I would pinch every penny. If he wept when drunk—and only when drunk—I would not let myself weep at all. If he roared at the Little League umpire for calling my pitches balls, I would throw nothing but strikes. Watching him flounder and rage, I came to dread the loss of control. I would go through life without making anyone mad. I vowed never to put in my mouth or veins any chemical that would banish my everyday self. I would never make a scene, never lash out at the ones I loved, never hurt a soul. Through hard work, relentless work, I would achieve something dazzling—in the classroom, on the basketball floor, in the science lab, in the pages of books—and my achievement would distract the world's eyes from his humiliation. I would become a worthy sacrifice, and the smoke of my burning would please God.

It is far easier to recognize these twists in my character than to undo them. Work has become an addiction for me, as drink was an addiction for my father. Knowing this, my daughter gave me a placard for the wall: WORKAHOLIC. The labor is endless and futile, for I can no more redeem myself through work than I could redeem my father. I still panic in the face of other people's anger, because his drunken temper was so terrible. I shrink from causing sadness or disappointment even to strangers, as though I were still concealing the family shame. I still notice every twitch of emotion in the faces around me, having learned as a child to read the weather in faces, and I blame myself for their least pang of unhappiness or anger. In certain moods I blame myself for everything. Guilt burns like acid in my veins.

\* \* \*

I am moved to write these pages now because my own son, at the age of ten, is taking on himself the griefs of the world, and in particular the griefs of his father. He tells me that when I am gripped by sadness he feels responsible; he feels there must be something he can do to spring me from depression, to fix my life. And that crushing sense of responsibility is exactly what I felt at the age of ten in the face of my father's drinking. My son wonders if I, too, am possessed. I write, therefore, to drag into the light what eats at me—the fear, the guilt, the shame—so that my own children may be spared.

I still shy away from nightclubs, from bars, from parties where the solvent is alcohol. My friends puzzle over this, but it is no more peculiar than for a man to shy away from the lions' den after seeing his father torn apart. I took my own first drink at the age of twenty-one, half a glass of burgundy. I knew the odds of my becoming an alcoholic were four times higher than for the sons of non-alcoholic fathers. So I sipped warily.

I still do—once a week, perhaps, a glass of wine, a can of beer, nothing stronger, nothing more. I listen for the turning of a key in my brain.

# TOYS IN THE ATTIC
## *An Ars Poetica Under the Influence*

### Chase Twichell

A poem is a portrait of consciousness. It's a recording of the motions of a mind in time, a mind communicating to others the experience of its own consciousness. When I read or write a poem, I'm trying to open a window between my mind and the minds of others. Poetry is written for others. But it's also a study of the self, which is a private kind of work.

Already I've had to use the troublesome words 'consciousness', 'mind', and 'self,' which are approximate and overlapping in their definitions because the thing they describe is a slippery animal. Buddhism has a useful all-purpose name for what I am: a sentient being, but even this label doesn't account for the persistent evidence suggesting that I am a unique and identifiable individual and can move as such through time. I want to explore this nexus of words–this atom of consciousness, mind, and self–by thinking about depression, from which I've suffered all my life, and its relation to poetry. For fifteen years I've lived with psychoactive drugs in my brain, among them Ambien, Celexa, Desyrel, Effexor, Elavil, Pamelor, Paxil, Serzone, Triavil, Valium, Wellbutrin, and Xanax, my Knights of the Round Table. I've studied the properties of each drug in the laboratories of my mind and body, and have made some unsettling but ultimately consoling discoveries concerning the nature of the self and its language. One is that the animal is slippery because it's mutable. It travels light, moving from drug to drug as if from country to country. The traveler learns that in all those foreign places the same language is spoken, precise and unadorned but also playful. It's the language I want for my poems because it's the language of my consciousness, my little piece of the flux, which happens to be something I fine-tune with psychopharmaceuticals.

In one of my earliest memories, I'm standing looking down into a storm drain, in which my younger sister is crouching. We're playing zoo, and she's the animal. I'm watching the elder sister, me, shove the heavy grate back over the opening. I'm slightly behind myself, like a shadow, a sensation I used to call "the eyes behind the eyes." In another memory, I'm about eight, reading in bed when my mother comes in to tell me that my dog, hit by a car the day before, has died at the vet's. I put my face in my hands, a self-conscious and exaggerated expression of sorrow. My first impulse is to act the part of a grieving child. I *am* a grieving child, of course, but the real grief is inaccessible to me at that moment. In its place is a calm, numb kind of consciousness, out of which I can fake the expected responses. I'm also playing my mother's words over and over in my head—she's said the dog's name, adding a *y* so that Centime (French poodle, French name) ends up *Centimey*, something my mother has never called her before. *Centimey died last night.* That *y* tells me a thousand things, among them that I am not completely inside myself the way I'm supposed to be.

The theme of third grade was Ancient Egypt. The teacher described how Howard Carter, excavating the Valley of the Kings for the first time, powered his steam-engines by burning legions of "lesser" mummies. No doubt this lurid detail was meant to enliven the study of history, but the irony of the dead digging up the dead struck me as contrary to the natural order of things, and I told the child psychiatrist about it. Dr. C. was a slow-moving, gentle, elderly woman who gave me a series of Rorschach tests. I said that the butterfly, the obvious one they show you to get you started, was a dead angel, and that another, blatantly phallic, was a tree split by lightning. The doctor had asked me to secretly clink minds with her, but I saw through the ruse. Outside myself as always, the watcher, the *modifier*, I lied to her in order to dramatize my pain, but also to keep her at a distance. I knew I wasn't normal—at school there was clear glass between me and the playground, me and my young fellow humans. I was the feral cat that slunk in and out of the garage at night, not the house pet asleep at the foot of the bed. I slept in my clothes and climbed down the drainpipe like a boy. But there was a joy that came with that loneliness. It was poetry, proof of a companion consciousness. As far back as I can remember, I recognized its language as my own.

What happens in depression, for reasons that are still unknown, is that the limbic-diencephalic system malfunctions. The biochemical chain reaction that results is extremely complicated, much of it still hypothetical. What is known is that certain neurotransmitters (especially serotonin and norepinephrine) do not work properly, causing a disruption in the flow of information between nerve cells. It's like a game of telephone; the message gets lost as it travels, eventually affecting cellular metabolism, hormone balance, and the circadian system, the internal clock that determines cycles of rest and activity. This translates into disturbances of mood, sleep, hunger, sex, memory formation, physical energy, hormone secretion (especially cortisol, the "fight or flight" chemical), and body temperature. As Dr. Demitri Papolos summarizes it, "Recent advances in the neurosciences are gradually revealing the central nervous system to look more and more like an interactive network of oscillating nuclei that exchange information across spatial and temporal boundaries that are modifiable by experience." *Across spatial and temporal boundaries that are modifiable by experience*—that's the part I'm trying to understand.

In my mid-thirties, which happens to be the average age of onset for clinical depression, I began shooting in the dark, as my doctor put it: searching through trial and error for a drug that would cure what ailed me with as few side effects as possible. Some of them make you dream, every night, the kind of dream you hate to wake from, rich and important-feeling. Others keep you skittering along the surface of sleep as if a car alarm were going off somewhere in the neighborhood, but not in your street. Some make you black out if you stand up too fast, or glue your tongue to the roof of your mouth. One cures migraines, another exacerbates them. All of them affect the way in which the brain processes language. It's not something a person uninterested in words might notice, except for maybe a bit of tip-of-the-tongue syndrome, but to me it's obvious that my relation to language has been subtly affected. Before the long parade of drugs, words were like water—all I had to do was dip my mind and it would come up brimming with new excitements. I always thought of this ability as a "gift," a part of my being. Now, the river of words flows around me as it always has, but I write as a translator, slightly outside the boundaries of my original language, fluent but no longer a native speaker. It's hard to explain. It feels like a new part of my brain has learned language, and the old part has atrophied. Put another way, it feels like a new self has displaced the old one. Maybe this sensation is just a physical metaphor for what the anti-depressants do, I don't know, but I've come to see that this death of imaginary self (along with its language) is not necessarily a hindrance to my work, though it took me years to stop trying to call my "gift" back from its grave. Its loss functions exactly as form does in poetry: if the door's locked, try a window.

What if the Self *is* a fiction of the hypothalamus? Aside from the uncomfortable inference that I may be nothing but a poorly-mixed cocktail of brain chemicals, this disturbing idea sounds like Zen, and also like science fiction. In the film *The Matrix,* a cyber-jockey called Neo (Keanu Reeves) is drafted by the underground to help bring about the downfall of the Matrix, a mutant computer program born of artificial intelligence, which has turned the human race into slaves. The "real world," based on urban America sometime early in the twenty-first century, is in fact computer-generated, a gilded cage for the population, which is unaware of the illusion that controls it. It's up to Neo and his new friends to reveal the truth, which, unhappily, turns out to be that the actual time is numerous centuries later than heretofore thought, and consists of a single surviving human city near the core of the earth, where there is still heat, and where the memory of freedom is kept alive by generations of escapees. I mention this particular science fiction because as a metaphor it expresses the essence of the Buddha's teaching: Life is suffering. Full of craving, we try to cling to illusion, the flux. What we experience as our "self" is a mental projection, a changeable idea; to see the world as it is, we must forget the self. Forgetting the self means realizing its true nature, which is that the boundary between it and the world is imaginary. This is why Zen is said to be a study of the self.

Well, if the self is a fiction, then whose fiction is it? What consciousness determines how The Fiction should be feeling? What if The Fiction finds the magic wand of psychopharmacology among the toys in the attic? As the twentieth century ends, I can take a single daily pill that elevates my mood, improves my ability to concentrate, and redesigns the architecture of my sleep. Humankind has always tinkered with consciousness, of course, but recent advances in neurobiology have made it possible to do so with extraordinary specificity, especially considering that much of the current knowledge rests on vast hypotheticals. But however the illusion of self is born, whether out of anger, ignorance, and greed, or trouble in the neurotransmitters, it's that unstable mental projection that makes language, and in whose voice I'm doomed to speak. It's a phantom who swallows that scored pink oval each night, and a phantom who writes my poems.

Of all human languages, poetry is the most powerful and precise, even more so than mathematics, since poetry can account for math's logic but math cannot account for poetry's. This is a tanka by Saito Mokichi (1882–1953):

*from where*
*a red tomato*
*lies rotting*
*I am only*
*a few steps away*

The demotion of the pronoun to the relative position puts the tomato in the position of the absolute. They have become "like the foot before and the foot behind in walking." This is also the relation of the poet to the poem. The language of poetry is the means by which one human consciousness speaks most intimately, directly, and precisely to others. Yet it is also an empty mirror, if I tell the truth of what I see. To me, the pleasure of this poem lies in its disquieting perspective, which enacts the self-dissolving.

It's hard to imagine what my relation to language might have been had I not been born with the genetic predisposition for depression. Studies of twins, both identical and fraternal, show that affective disorders are indeed hereditary. Depression (and manic depression) tend to run in families—on both sides, in my case. In all likelihood I'll have to take psychoactive drugs for the rest of my life. I'll try the new ones as they come on the market. I'll inhabit subtly new selves, which will think in subtly new language. This no longer threatens my understanding of what it means to be a "self," or to write poems, though sometimes when I'm tired I long for a different kind of consciousness that might let me rest in the illusion of a unique personhood. I used to think that everyone, especially poets, wanted to understand the true nature of the self, to know what it means to be conscious, and thus to think deeply about death. But most poems I read are about other things. This no longer surprises me, since the death of the self is not something the self likes to think too much about, fiction or not. Rereading *On the Road* the other day, I came across this passage in which Sal Paradise riffs on a dream he's had: *"Something, someone, some spirit was pursuing all of us across the desert of life and was bound to catch us before we reached heaven. Naturally, now that I look back on it, this is only death: death will overtake us before heaven. The one thing that we yearn for in our living days, that makes us sigh and groan and undergo sweet nauseas of all kinds, is the remembrance of some lost bliss that was probably experienced in the womb and can only be reproduced (though we hate to admit it) in death. But who wants to die? In the rush of events I kept thinking about this in the back of my mind; I told it to Dean and he instantly recognized it as the mere simple longing for pure death; and because we're all of us never in life again, he, rightly, would have nothing to do with it, and I agreed with him then."*

I admire the way these sentences replicate the self's reflexive refusal of this knowledge, and the shrewdness of that last word, *then*, which admits the ultimate failure of the maneuver.

To me, consciousness is the supremely interesting thing, and poetry the ultimate art of self-annihilation. This is not a contradiction. Consciousness is the lens through which I either see the road to death, or do not, if the lens has cataracts, and the biggest, most opaque cataract of them all is the fiction of the self as a static uniqueness unassailable by time. I want to write in the language of the flux I know myself to be: physical and chemical, immortal and non-existent. That's why, when language comes to me or I go to language, I always meet it somewhere outside of my self. From where a red tomato lies rotting I am only a few steps away.

# CANCELLED ELEGY

## Molly Peacock

Draw a bath without bubbles. Warm water
with a slightly yellowish cast. (Imagine
life as a window to itself.) No food for
two days before— all evacuated. Sin
to let a big mess spoil it. (Your bowels go
into spasm when you die.) Step in. Put
your head back on the ledge. Place the blade so
it's easily reached. When relaxed and warm, cut
across each wrist beneath the water's skin
and let blood flow like the ancient Romans.
But doesn't a bath defy self-denial?
Clear, but unlike glass, it laps. Nothing
can be cut from it. There is your frail
body in the tub's womb, where you feel pain,
my darling thing, because you feel warm.

# PRETTY RED STRIPES

## Linda Gray Sexton

Smoking a cigarette, I sat in my car in the parking lot at the edge of Oak Manor Park. Valentine's Day had come to California and there was a warm wet rain streaking down my windshield. It was a year and counting since my suicide attempt. I had been without Jim for all that time, if I counted his departure from when he began to withdraw and shut me out. The rain was having a curious, prosaic effect on me: it summoned up old memories of my mother and how she had toilet trained me by running the tap.

But I wasn't there to think about the past. I fastened my mind on more recent events.

The large area of well-tended grass was bounded by a fence of lattice design, and enormous oak trees waved their leaves in the wind like women shaking out their hair. Immaculately kept, the profusion of shrubbery gave off an air of serenity, as if someone ought to be playing croquet next to the gazebo. Before my separation from Jim, this was where I walked my two Dalmatians, Rhiannon and Tia. Now I had only Gulliver, and I never brought him here, a place too haunted by their memory.

After I had been discharged from the hospital in December of 1997, I had at least tried to keep both the thoughts of suicide and my internal voice tamped down under a cheerful surface, tried to keep up with my friends and persevere with my activities. But slowly everything normal began to drop away. I missed Jim as fiercely as I had supposed I would.

In my mind, suicide was obviously off-limits, never to be experienced again, but as the months passed, moving into the new year, I acted increasingly upon the education I had received at the hospital: Cutting 101.

For the eight weeks following the anniversary of my first suicide attempt, my thoughts had turned obsessively on the axis of death; the colors of survival blanked out the red hot touch of passion, the blue of cool comforting hands, the celery green of that new spring's energy. The world was black and white. And so, that day in the park that had once been ours, I ruminated about the terrible engulfing dark of Rhiannon and Tia's death; I wanted to cry, but could not. Jim was gone, my mother was gone, two of my dogs were gone. And despite my mother's promise on that wintry day when my kitten had died, "living on" in my heart was not nearly enough.

Back before my empty weekend days began to extend themselves into some kind of twilight sleep, back before I'd thought I could escape the legacy by simply looking away from that abyss into which I could so easily fall, I was like the drunk who thinks he can get clean simply by avoiding the bottle. Yet, here I was, returning to a place that was familiar and filled with good memories. Sadness prevailed nonetheless. I felt only grief at discovering myself once again, right here, right where the dogs and I had been so united.

And so I promised myself, like a drug addict, that I would take only one bump of death that rainy day.

And this was why I had sought out such a solitary location; it suited my intention, a small treat right there in the parking lot.

I had become a true cutter, feeling better each time I sliced into my skin. I had already cut myself earlier that week, despite the fact that after my first bout with cutting following the suicide attempt, I had promised Ben that I would never do it again.

"Why do you hurt yourself this way?" asked Ben Berns.

"It's a way of letting the poison out. Taking control again." Desperately I tried to make him understand how I felt. "It makes the voice in my head shut up. To bleed is a way of knowing you're alive."

He shook his head; he plainly did not understand the miraculous power cutting had to make me feel better. Ben drew up a contract requiring my signature, handwritten on a yellow-lined piece of paper that I carried in my wallet. In it, I promised that I wouldn't try to hurt myself, not even to the smallest degree, because he warned me he would not act as a therapist to anyone who was actively self-mutilating. I signed, but I knew in that moment, exactly then, that it was not realistic to believe that I could simply decide to stay in sufficient control; I could not promise that I would abstain from this kind of enjoyment—no matter how small it was— and so I lied. Death and its near misses had a power all their own. It seemed to me that the urge to cut controlled me, rather than the reverse. The punishment for breaking my contract with Ben would be the forfeiture of therapy with him—but in that moment, I didn't care.

I had also promised him, specifically, that should I cut myself, I would confess immediately. I knew, of course, that following such revelations he would refuse to see me any longer and I would be alone once again. The consolation prize would be that he would help me find a new therapist. These conditions did not promote honesty between us; his rigorous rules simply drove my behavior underground. The price for restraining myself was too high—just as the price of cutting was in and of itself very high. The guilt over lying to him paled next to the urge to bleed myself. And so, that week and the week before, I had broken our contract and then remained silent in our sessions, bringing to a close the code of truth that must exist between therapist and patient for true work to continue.

For four days that week, the threat of his withdrawal had kept me from cutting again, but that day in the park, the buzz wanted to get out, and I couldn't hold it back any longer. I didn't care what he would do or that I might be required to lie, or what I would have to do in order to cover the demon of my action. I was wresting control in my internal chaos. I had decided to cut my ankles because the wounds would be easier to hide: bandaged wrists would alert Ben immediately.

It was my first time with a razor blade.

An hour ago at the hardware store, I had bought a transparent plastic container of ten, each wrapped in brown paper, each with an edge sharp as a wasp's sting. Carefully I unwrapped the creased paper jacket in which the first lay, savoring in advance the ready-made high it would bring, as if I were sitting down to a roast beef dinner.

I could still feel the high anticipation as I settled into the cushion of my seat and pulled my ankle onto my lap, adroitly fashioning a lotus position beneath the steering wheel. I made a light test run. After a second, delicate ruby beads strung out along my skin. And then a deep breath before I made the first straight controlled shot, its length just two thumb's lengths, maybe a few inches. The sound the blade made as it moved through this level of my skin was something like cloth ripping; it made me grind my lip between my teeth. On the inside of my ankle, the straight white lips of the cut opened and there was a quick rush of blood from the wound.

"Nice color," said my inner voice. "Go back and do it again, a little deeper this time."

I felt the next sharp sting and took a deep breath at the pain; my face flushed. In my life, in that moment, nothing was happening except this. I hated doing it. I loved doing it. I paused then; tears watered in my eyes as I trembled in the blank purity of the instant. Exhaled then, a long blow outward. Flooded with pleasure. With my windshield running rain and the inside windows steaming up, I was in a cocoon. Unobserved. My despair seeped out, if only for a moment. I was bringing Death close, drawing him deep within the circle of my arms.

\* \* \*

I had time to ruminate between cuts, and my mind tipped backwards, to the days of the other more, many more, pleasurable things: to the walks I had taken with the dogs here. My family had had five Dalmatians and one litter of eight puppies when I was growing up, and all of us believed that dogs were something to celebrate. Dogs kept us alive, sometimes even when my mother was making a bid for death. In February of 1966, she wrote a poem called "Live," using as inspiration our new puppies, who bleated out little hungry cries as they crawled around, searching for the teat.

When Jim and I moved to California, we at last had a large backyard; with the children in school full-time, it was easy to reinstate the happy legacy of Dalmatians in my life with the demands of a cute puppy. In this way did a one-year-old show-quality bitch Rhiannon, named after a Welsh witch and the Fleetwood Mac song, become ours. I was disappointed that she wasn't a puppy, but we bonded almost immediately and I put my desire for a dog in its earliest months aside.

For the next several years, I took lessons in dog handling and obedience training two days a week, practicing on the back lawn every night after supper, while Jim threw the baseball around with the boys. We spoiled Rhiannon shamelessly, and slowly she developed into—as parlance in the trade called it—a "special" dog: one who had rare depths of understanding for the humans who owned her. As we practiced in the backyard, I realized that I hadn't had such fun since summer camp, where I loved to ride and show horses.

That year, I brought a new puppy into our home. The calm of my two years alone with Rhiannon was shattered by the arrival of a rambunctious bombshell, Tia, just twelve weeks old. The kids were thrilled.

When Rhiannon turned two, I carefully chose a mate for her, putting genetics first to make sure I had a litter of lively but quiet, obedient dogs, those who would defy the ubiquitous stereotype that Dals were hyperactive. We sent Rhiannon to Minneapolis to be bred and decided we might perhaps take another pup from the litter, scheduled for January. Jim had rolled his eyes at the idea of a three dog household, but I wanted a male this time around. As the time of Rhiannon's whelping drew near, I laid out the instruments, the towels, the scale, the rickrack that would encircle every puppy's neck as he or she arrived so that I would be able to track both weights and well-being.

One by one the puppies slid out, still encased in their watery blue bubbles. My hands shook and nausea erupted at the bloody mess before me. A particular smell, coppery and pungent, pervaded the warm room but I couldn't have named it—something that hovered, perhaps, between life and death.

In a few moments all the nausea and the shaking of my hands stopped, as I lost myself in helping Rhiannon open the membranes. I tied off the umbilical cords and then weighed the pups as they came. It was an experience I would never forget. I held beginning life cradled between the palms of my hands, and perhaps this was the reason I had done it to begin with. Perhaps I had needed to rediscover the magic my entire family felt when our litter of puppies pulled my mother away from her instinct to die, and returned to her a desire to live.

She whelped eight puppies while I was alone in the house early that weekday January afternoon. Nearly all were girls. Eventually I would place "Ashley," the most striking female of the litter, into a show home, from which I could take her to dog shows. Over time, my co-owner, Pat Maciejewski, would become a deep and valued friend, with whom I shared much joy and laughter as we toted the dogs around in her sleek R.V. Later, I would breed Ashley to my friend Dawn's best stud. When her litter arrived there was a beautiful boy I immediately claimed as my own, and in this way Gulliver joined our household.

Things were not relaxed between Rhiannon and Tia, however, and soon we were locked into a downward spiral. Though the two dogs initially got along well, when Tia reached adolescence, she made a bid for being the head of the pack, and the two of them also became jealous of their time with me. Or perhaps, it was just that Rhiannon couldn't tolerate another puppy who was claiming some of my attention as I began to train Gulliver for the ring.

One night Rhiannon and Tia grew aggressive over a dropped bagel, and went at each other in a quick, sudden confrontation. It was a dance of unrecognizable, unanticipated hatred. They growled and rose quickly to their haunches, locking on, muzzle to muzzle. When they broke for a moment to establish a new drip, Gabe and I, terrified, managed to drag them into separate rooms. Oozing red gouges and gashes marked the snow of their coats.

After our trip to the vet, I called a recommended behaviorist in desperation. I was afraid to let the dogs together again. She made a house call, and established order. From that point on, as instructed, we hung from every doorknob trash bags chock full of soda cans that were filled with pennies—the loud rattling that came when a bag was shaken was one of the only things to which the fighting dogs would respond. I worked with her several times a week, practicing submission exercises so that the dogs would look to me for their cues, rather than relying on their own instincts as to who was the leader.

Six months went by and it seemed as if they had relented in their sudden hatred of each other—but then, suddenly another fight: Tia's teeth missed Rhiannon's left eye by inches; Rhiannon needed twenty stitches for the slashes in her muzzle, through which blood bubbled as she struggled to breathe.

The gateway had opened. And so it went, fight after fight, the behaviorist arriving, new electric shock collars strapped on, the terrible hatred between them continuing. At last it seemed there was no help for us. Yet I was determined to keep both of them, determined that my love for them would conquer their hatred for each other, just as I had once thought that my love for mother would conquer her hatred of life.

We were counseled by the behaviorist: never put your hands into the middle of a dog fight. She knew people who had lost fingers, or even, a hand. Gabe in particular grew terrified, and we learned to keep the dogs apart, each confined to her own crate and allowed out only when the other was safely shut away. We lived with an expanding fear that billowed outward into our lives.

There were a total of eight fights, with the bills mounting into the thousands. I didn't remember all the wounds. I didn't remember all the surgical packs, the endless visits to the behaviorist. I just remembered each dog's face, so important to me, so destined to endure in my heart.

"If they have another fight," the behaviorist told me at last, "you'll have to put them down."

It was those words, catching me with a gripping nausea, that made me realize how bad things were. I asked her, with desperation, for her opinion on placements, but she shook her head. Even if I could find them other homes, I could not be certain they would be dependably safe—with other dogs, or even with people who might get their hands into the middle of a fight. I asked around, desperately seeking another solution, scrolling through the pages of names in my membership booklets of the Dalmatian clubs. Not a single other breeder would take on even one of them.

But then, luckily perhaps, a year and a half of peace passed and I relaxed. I got sloppy. The shaker cans were relegated to the closets. And, at last, the dogs slept together on the same bed again, ate side by side again, romped and played and even "mock-fought" from one end of our green acre to the other, under supervision. At six, I supposed, Rhiannon had mellowed. That autumn, when I brought Gulliver into our family, interestingly enough, both other dogs perked up with a youngster around. They had come to an understanding, it seemed.

Hubris led me to complacence, to the belief that I could overcome their instinct for the jugular. And I was also very preoccupied: I had reached the point when I finally understood my mother's wish to die, and saw that the wish had at last become my own. I believed that if I understood, I ought to be able to control it all. I got cocky. With the dogs' lives as well as with my own.

In late November, just before my suicide attempt, I came home from shopping with Gabe and let the dogs loose from their crates. For no reason I could discern, Rhiannon came full blast into the room, snarling and ready, and Tia met her full bore.

In a fury, they fought across the bedroom and knocked over a table, a lamp and a chair. The blood began to spray across the white sheets. I couldn't stop them. Both Gabe and I stood to one side as instructed, unable to intervene, terrified and useless. I turned to the door for the shaker can bag that should have been hanging on the knob but was not.

At last Tia squirmed under the bed. Rhiannon stood panting, her legs splayed, her left ear torn from one side of the pinna to the other, hanging on by only a thin thread of tissue. Blood dripped down the side of her muzzle and onto the carpet.

I bundled them into their crates in the van and sped down the highway to the vet. I didn't want to face the inevitable but my inner voice was virtually clamoring with the obvious. Once in the office, Rhiannon lay down beside me where I sat on the linoleum, and snuggled her head deep into my lap, despite the pain she must have felt from her nearly detached ear. She looked up at me with the dark soulful eyes that had first convinced me to take her home, those dark eyes that had always relied on me to protect and care for her. The blood pooled on the floor.

The vet wound the tourniquet around Rhiannon's leg and located the pulse of her vein beneath her taut white coat. The tech handed over the syringe. My dog looked up at me, right into my eyes, still trusting, and I numbly repressed the words that would stop everything. The minutes had slowed and it was hard to breathe. My hands shook. And so, I simply held my dog because holding her was all that was left for me to do. Her tail was wagging, hard, left to right and back again, but suddenly, like a motor running down, it slowed, and then she was gone from me, away from the touch of my hands and the love in my face. Her eyes stared into mine, empty. I had killed her. Death was in my life, this time in my hands, once more.

* * *

Sitting in the car with my razor blade that day in February, I remembered Rhiannon's face with longing, and drew another line across my ankle and watched it bleed, using a tissue to sop up the blood. There were several such bloodied tissues scattered on the passenger seat of my car, and I felt proud that I had been able to cut deeply enough to need to staunch the bleeding. My inner voice was bitter and loud about my inability to keep my dogs alive, and I had no answer to gain relief except to draw another cut.

The bright red of the small perfect incisions on my ankles reminded me of the way the dogs had drawn the blood that stained their snowy coats. I had killed them just before I had tried to kill myself by cutting my wrists, blood blossoming then into the water of the bath. Blood for blood. November to December: the arrival of death twice in the span of a month.

And yet, where they had died, I had failed.

Fourteen months later, in the car now, punishment beckoned. I hated myself for what I had done to them. I tugged my ankle closer and bent over my work, using the forward edge of the blade and following with the center, just as smoothly as a skater cuts circles on fresh ice. I'd dig to China maybe. Down through the layers. Here was sinew. Here was fat, muscle, tendon. What secret lay hidden, here in the strata of my body?

When I was finished, my ankles buzzed but my insides did not and there was relief in this. Still, a sense of let-down suffused me: The pretty tidiness of my cuts disappointed after all.

I sat back in the seat, my sense of dissatisfaction growing: for this I would have to powder my wounds, wear thick socks, create a lie for Ben. While cutting might suffice for a while, I could see that one day soon I would grow bored with these pretty red stripes, set back to back like the careful ruler lines of a long ago grammar school copybook. After a while, I would have to get back to the big time.

# LAST DAY OUT

## Sue William Silverman

Every Thursday at noon I have sex with Rick in room #213 of the Rainbow Motel. Today, even though I promised my therapist I wouldn't come here again, I pull into the lot and park beside Rick's black Ford Bronco. I cut the engine and air conditioner and listen to stillness, to nothing, to heat. Sunrays splinter the windshield. Heat from the pavement rises, stifling, around the car, around me. No insects flutter in the brittle grass next to the lot. Trees don't rustle with bird wings. A neon rainbow, mute and colorless by day, arcs over a sign switched to vacancy. Only the little girl from India, daughter of the motel owner, invigorates the stasis. Holding a string tied to a green balloon, she races down the diving board and leaps into the swimming pool. With the windows closed, I can't hear the splash. If she laughs, I can't hear this, either. For a moment she disappears. The balloon gaily sways above the water. The girl pops to the surface. She begins the game again.

The girl's energy exhausts me—as much as the stagnation of neon, air, time. I close my eyes. Still, I sense no darkness, no cool shadows, no relief from the scorching Georgia heat. Rather, a harsh light, white as a sheet, penetrates my lids as if I am caught in an unforgiving glare.

I worry the girl by the pool will see me. She's too young to know what I do here in the Rainbow Motel.

I should leave. I should leave here now. I should drive home and rinse pink gloss from my lips, wipe mascara from my lashes, change out of my too-short skirt and too-tight black lace blouse. I should cook a nourishing dinner for my husband. I should grasp the balloon and let it waft me across the sky, far from my implacable need for men. Dangerous men. Not physically dangerous. Emotionally dangerous. These men see me just as an object, a body. They are men incapable of love—even though I endlessly, addictively, try to convince myself that sex at noon for an hour with a married man has to be the real thing, must be love.

So I can't leave here. I need Rick. One last time. One last high. One last fix.

I should drive to the rehab unit and find my therapist right now.

Pausing outside the door of room #213, I hear the television: a car crash, urgent voices. I turn the knob and lock it behind me. Rick lies on the sheet smoking a cigarette, the remote beside him. He inhales. Exhales. Smoke swirls. I watch it disperse. An ash drifts onto the pillowcase. He doesn't notice. He hasn't stopped watching me since I entered.

He leans over and stubs out the cigarette. He clicks off the television and beckons me closer. A gold necklace nestles in his blond hair, a rich glitter of gold on gold as if chain mail emblazons his chest. Lying beside him, I curl short strands of his hair around my finger as if, in all this incandescence, we radiate love. His Eau Sauvage cologne is the only scent in the world I will ever need or want. I close my eyes, drenched in it. In him. I must feel Rick's touch, a drug surging through veins, trancing me as I urgently swallow oblivion and ether. Sex, a sweet amnesiac. The elixir drains through my body, thin as a flame. I crave this, need him-or You, Man, whoever You are-until I'm blissfully satiated...

Is this bliss?

I open my eyes. He's leaning over me, his palm on the pillow beside my head. I can hear the second hand of his watch ticking beside my ear. His breath numbs the hollow at the base of my neck. Sweat gathers on his temples. The necklace taps my chin as he fucks me. A gift from his wife? I wonder. He kisses me. Strokes me. But this is just a repetition of all the other times with Rick. Nothing unusual. Just the basics. Routine sex. He doesn't even bother to try to impress me with fancy positions like Crushing Spices. Flower in Bloom. Dear to Cupid. Just the missionary position. Sometimes sixty-nine-but all Rick wants is to get the job done. Quickly.

Not that I mind. I don't do this for pleasure. I do this for love.

Except I feel a damp chill between my shoulder blades— thinking of all the times my spine has creased this mattress—so many mattresses. The second hand ticks. He pushes up on his elbows, his head above mine. He glances down, focusing more on my torso than on me. I hug him tighter. Feel *me*. See *me*. I touch his throat with the tip of my tongue. His skin tastes like salt water and indigo. My limbs feel weighted with leaden male gravity. Smothered. I feel as if I sink below water, far beneath a night sea.

Can't I understand that this, what we do here, has only, ever, been numbed emotions of familiar strangers, fucking? Why can't I accept the difference between this and love? How can love be two bodies wrapped in a sheet that's singed by careless cigarettes, here, in a room with plastic curtains, tin ashtrays, base metal, stained carpet, bad alchemy, artificial air, and a television promoting the same pornographic movies every hour on the hour? Here in a room when, by one o'clock, Rick looks depleted, the blue of his eyes seeming to have bled beneath the skin.

Rick retrieves a Polaroid camera from a small gym bag. He aims it at me, still lying in bed, my head propped on the pillow. He jokes: "Smile." I stare straight into the lens. In the flash I am dazed, as if I've imploded.

I know he needs this photo like a stash, a memento, in order to remember while I'm gone.

Tomorrow morning I am to enter an inpatient treatment facility where I must remain sexually sober for twenty-eight long days. I don't want to go. But if I don't, I'll remain addicted to sex, to men, to dangerous men. My therapist, whom I've been seeing for almost a year, says I must go. For out here, loose in the world, I haven't been able to stop on my own.

Rick goes to shower.

Pieces of my body surface in the Polaroid. My neck down to my knees. I want to be pleased. For only when my body is desired do I feel beautiful, powerful, loved. Except I don't feel powerful, loved, or whole now. I feel shy, embarrassed, exhausted. Less. Yes, as if I am less than a body. For right now my body seems to exist only in this Polaroid.

For months, like a mantra, my therapist has told me, "These men are killing you." I don't know if he means emotionally, spiritually, or physically. I don't ask. He explains that I confuse sex with love, compulsively repeating this destructive pattern with one man after another. I do this because as a girl I learned that sex is love from my father, the first dangerous man who sexually misloved me.

"I thought the intensity with Rick must be love," I say.

"The intensity is an addict's 'high,'" my therapist says. "Not love." To numb the shame and fear associated both with the past and with my current sexual behavior, I medicate, paradoxically, by using sex, he explains. "But sometimes that 'high' stops working. Usually after a scary binge."

Like last Thursday at Rick's house.

Rick and I didn't meet at the Rainbow Motel. His son was home from school with the flu, and Rick took the day off from work to stay with him. Rick and I undressed in the bedroom he shares with his wife, while his son slept in his room down the hall. The house was hushed. The door to the bedroom locked. But then I heard a small sound: his son crying.

Rick heard him, too. I expected Rick to rush to him. We wouldn't have sex. Instead, we would read his son a story. *I* wanted to read his son a story. Give him a glass of water. *I* wanted to give him a glass of water. Press a washcloth to his cheeks. I paused, sure I felt his son's fever, damp and urgent. He needed his father.

His father didn't need him.

Rick's hands tugged at belts and zippers: hurry. We will do this... even though his son might get out of bed, knock on the door, see me leave his parents' bedroom. What I then forced myself to know was that this, this one careless act of sex, was more important to Rick than his son. And because I, too, couldn't say no, because I feared Rick would leave me if I refused him sex, I began to know, had to accept, that sex was more important to me, too. In a moment of clarity I realized that, while the sober part of me wanted to attend his son, a tangled, humid, inescapable part stopped me. Time stalled: with Rick's hands forever on his belt buckle; with my fingers always on the zipper of my skirt.

And a moment later, I no longer heard his son crying.

The next therapy session I told my therapist, Ted, about Rick's son. More: I confessed that I'd been secretly meeting Rick for weeks without telling him, Ted. I couldn't stop. Before I'd left Ted's office, he called the inpatient unit where he worked and scheduled my admittance. He told me it wasn't possible for him to work with clients who showed up for a session "drunk" or "hungover." He could no longer see me as an outpatient; he could only help me in the rehab unit. "To have real feelings, you have to be sexually sober," he said. "Not numbed out." Afraid to be abandoned by Ted, beginning to accept the emotional destructiveness of my behavior, I agreed to go.

Now, as I cross the motel parking lot, dingy afternoon light fuses my blouse to my sweaty back. All I want is to sleep it off. My footsteps sound hollow. My mouth tastes contaminated, metallic. The little girl and her green balloon are gone. Without her energy, the pool is a flat, glassy sheen. Driving from the lot, I pass the neon sign, silently spelling "Rainbow Motel."

I should never return here; yet I can't imagine not meeting Rick every Thursday at noon. For what I do in room #213 is the only reason, I believe, a man would love me ... *what my father taught me was love.*

That evening my husband and I eat a silent dinner at the kitchen table. Andrew sits erect, solid, focused on a Braves baseball game on the portable television, while I hunch over my plate. Andrew takes angry bites of an overdone hamburger, the third one I fixed this week, and canned string beans, all I managed to prepare after returning from the motel. I nibble at an edge of hamburger and spear one bean onto my fork. I put it down without eating. Looking at all the food, I think I might be sick. Fumes from the motel seem to rise from the hem of my skirt. My body feels sticky and smudged. It feels unhealthy. Andrew seems not to see, pretends not to notice, this mess that is me. Or, yes, he notices. But he never asks questions. He is too afraid of the answers.

"Sorry about the dinner," I say.

He isn't angry about the affairs; he doesn't know about them. He's angry about my emotional disarray. He wants me to be industrious and smiling. Normal. I worry, even with therapy, I won't learn how to love him the way I should, won't learn how to act like a wife.

"I was wondering," I say, during a television commercial break, "maybe you could drive me over there tomorrow and help me get settled."

"I can't just not teach my classes." His fingers grip the fork.

I want to touch his hand, loosen the grip, warm our fingers.

"I need to finish grading papers." He pushes back his chair. "Remember to call your parents, tell them where you're going," he says. His six-foot body fills the doorway.

"I wouldn't know what to say if they call here looking for you."

I scrape my uneaten hamburger and beans into the garbage. Nothing to clean from Andrew's plate, only a smear of ketchup, a few bread crumbs. I squeeze Ivory liquid soap onto the sponge and wash several days' worth of dishes. With a Brillo pad I scour the long-encrusted broiler pan. I sprinkle Comet in the stained sink. I set Andrew's blue cereal bowl on the counter next to his coffee mug, ready for his breakfast in the morning. I want to do more: mop linoleum, polish hardwood floors. I want to try harder to please Andrew. I never can. There's always a distraction, always a Rick, or someone. Now, tonight, I feel the burden of calling my parents, the burden of going to the hospital, press against my back. I feel as if I've lost all my muscles.

I turn on the lamp in the living room and sit on our Victorian couch. I pick up the telephone and dial my parents' number. My mother answers on the second ring. Even though my parents know I'm in therapy, I've never said the word incest aloud in their presence. Whenever I visit, once or twice a year, we still eat dinner on pretty Wedgwood plates the way we always did. We are silently confused with each other, or else we speak as if no one heard my father turn the doorknob on all my childhood bedrooms ...never heard the door click shut all those nights.

Now I say to my mother that I have something important to tell her. There is a pause before she answers, "Sure, honey," then places her hand over the receiver. She calls to my father, who picks up the extension. "Hi, precious," he says to me.

I tell them there's nothing to worry about. I've just been depressed and need to go away for about a month. "I'll be at this treatment facility where my therapist works."

"I don't understand," my mother says. "I thought you said you've been doing so much better."

I have told them this lie. They are paying for my therapy sessions, and I want them to think they're getting their money's worth. Ironically, they want me to feel better even as they never ask why I need therapy in the first place.

"How do you know this therapist knows what he's doing?" my father says. "He doesn't know anything about you."

*This therapist* knows my life is out of control, I want to say. He knows I'm afraid to eat, can't feed my body. He knows I fuck men because it's what you taught me is love.

Father, this therapist knows everything. About you.

The back of my neck is sweaty, and I coil my hair around my fist. Quizzle, my cat, jumps on the couch and curls beside me.

I barely hear my voice. "He knows I don't know how to love right," I say.

"What kind of people would be in a place like that?" he says.

The more he speaks, the more weightless my head feels, the more sluggish my body. My stomach cramps: with hunger, with fear. I don't know if I can do this.

"People like me," I whisper.

"I won't hear about this," he says.

"Dad, wait. My therapist said he'll want to schedule a family session. I mean, I know you can't come down here, but we'll do it on the phone. Like a conference call."

"If he wants a meeting, tell him to send me an agenda."

"That's not exactly how it's done."

"Then how can I know what we're going to talk about?"

"What do you think we're going to talk about?"

The phone clicks.

I know we'll never have a family session, even on the phone.

"Mom?"

"I'm still here."

"You think he's really angry?"

"Can't you call him from the hospital without these therapists?"

My therapist has told me I'm to have no unsupervised contact with my father while in the hospital. No contact with Rick, either.

"How about I'll send you flowers?" she adds.

I don't want flowers. I don't want presents. All you give are presents. You gave me as a present. To your husband. By feigning illness and staying in bed, your eyes shut, the door closed, you could pretend not to notice how you made me available to your husband—a gift—a little-girl wife.

"Mother, I don't want flowers, I want..."

"What?"

The impossible: a real father; a mother who saw what she saw, knew what she knew. Even though the last time my father touched me sexually was when I left home for college some twenty-five years ago, it feels as if I've never left that home at all.

"Just to get better, I guess," I answer.

"Well, be sure to pack a warm robe and slippers," my mother says. "Bring plenty of vitamin C. You know how cold they keep those places." I am about to hang up when she adds, "Oh, and call your sister. She's doing so well in her new job."

I put down the phone and sink back into the velvet cushion on the couch. I grew up in pretty houses decorated with art objects my father bought on his many travels; how easily our family hid its secrets behind carved wood masks from Samoa, straw fans from Guam. How successful we seemed, with elegant tea sets from Japan, silk curtains from Hong Kong. Now Andrew and I have nice antiques, an Oriental rug, watercolor paintings. Things. I was raised to believe that if a family appears perfect, it must be perfect. I have tried to keep up appearances.

I open the door to Andrew's study. He doesn't look up. He is an English professor, and he sits at his desk grading student papers. I lean over his shoulder and wrap my arms around his chest. I tell him I called my parents, that my father hung up, that my mother worries I'll catch cold. He sighs, and doesn't put down his pencil.

I straighten and lean against his desk. Bookcases jammed with volumes by James Joyce, Thomas Pynchon, Tolstoy, Cervantes, Jane Austen, Derrida, Riffaterre, Kant, line the walls like thick insulation. He is writing a book of his own, evolved from his dissertation. I have typed the manuscript several times for him, several revisions. I have proofread it twice. Yet I only have a vague understanding of what it's about.

Even though I married Andrew for his cool distant silence—so different from my father's needy raging—now, this moment, I want to get his attention. I want to say: Look at me! I want to crack the silence of our marriage and reveal to him the complete reason my therapist says I must enter the hospital now: to be sequestered, quarantined, from men. But I can't tell Andrew. For I believe if he sees the real me, he'll leave me. All he knows for sure is that I'm entering treatment because what happened to me as a child caused an eating disorder and I hate food.

I turn, about to close the door to his study. "I'm sorry," is all I'm able to say. "You know?"

"Look, I'm sure it'll be fine," he says. "Call me when you get there. Let me know you made it okay."

Later I lie awake, where I sleep by myself, in a small second-story bedroom. The attic fan whooshes air from the basement up through the house and out the windows, out the vents in the gable. The house feels vacant. Andrew sleeps directly below me in a king-sized bed. I roll onto my stomach in my narrow bed and press my fingertips against the wood floor. I want to feel a quiet vibration from his breath. I want to tiptoe down the stairs and slip beneath the covers beside him. I want the scent of his freshly laundered sheets on my own body, his clean, strong hand to hold mine. I want to feel a reassuring, constant presence of this man labeled "husband." I don't know how. Ordinary married life is too tame and mild. I want to hold on to him, but Andrew, as well as our ten-year marriage, only skims the periphery of my senses.

Initially I moved in with Andrew because he asked me. I was searching for love, even though I was married to someone else at the time. But bored with my first marriage, I thought all I needed to be happy was to switch partners. After a divorce and living together about a year, Andrew and I decided to marry. The morning of our wedding, however, I awoke with a headache, my muscles stiff with the responsibility of maintaining a relationship: yes, too ordinary, committed, boring. Not as intense or exciting— not as short-lived—as a one-night stand or an affair. Scant weeks before the wedding I'd even come close to having sex with the president of a company where I was doing "temp" work for $4.50 an hour. I'm not sure why I said no to that president, except maybe this time I really wanted to make a stab at marriage.

I'd ordered my "wedding dress" out of a catalogue. It was a red cotton floral outfit, marked down to nineteen dollars.

Andrew urged me to buy something nicer. I couldn't.

How could I tell him I bought the dress because I felt marked down? How could I wear white or cream or tan when red is my true color?

Three-thirty in the morning. The silence of our house, our marriage, wells up around me. Night is a thick humid wall. I need a way out. I push back the sheet and retrieve a lavender wood box I've hidden for years in my closet. I sit on the floor. Inside the box is my stash—stuff hoarded for when I need a fix—these mementos of men almost as good as a real man. Letters, photos, jewelry, books, pressed flowers. A maroon cashmere scarf that an older married man gave me when I was a college student in Boston. I drape the scarf around my neck.

From my dresser I remove khaki shorts, underwear, socks, a few wrinkled T-shirts, a pair of gray sweats, and place them in my canvas suitcase. I slide my fingers along metal hangers in the closet. Short skirts. Silk and lacy blouses. Rainbow Motel blouses. I also own blazers and oxford shirts, professional clothes, from various past jobs, even though I am currently unemployed. Size-four dresses to clothe my anorexic body. Size-eight for when I'm eating. But little in this closet is appropriate for a hospital. On a shelf in the back I find an oversized white T-shirt with the stenciled message: stranded on the strand. It is so old the seams are splitting, the print fading. I bought it in Galveston, where I once lived, in an area called the Strand. I always read the message literally: I have felt stranded. Everywhere. I decide to wear it tomorrow.

I tuck the maroon scarf between the shirts in my suitcase.

Next to my bedroom is the bath. I collect deodorant, toothbrush, toothpaste, comb. No makeup. Not even lipstick for this new sober self I will try to create tomorrow. In the medicine cabinet is my supply of Gillette single-edged razor blades. Why not? The metal feels cool, comforting. The blades are to slice small cuts in my skin. How peaceful, whenever I drift into a trance of silver razors, obsessed with watching slivers of blood trail down my thighs. Small hurts always distract me from the larger hurts. Blood, starvation, promiscuity, are managed pain, meant to relieve larger, *un*manageable pain.

I slip a razor blade under the bar of Dove soap in my pink plastic soap dish and put it in my suitcase.

# THE BOTTOM

## Denise Duhamel

I stopped drinking on my way down the hill
to the liquor store when two guys pulled up
and tried to drag me into their pickup. I crossed the street
then ran in the opposite direction, puffing
against the incline. The stranger thrust into reverse
and, when I wouldn't talk to him,
threw a bag of McDonald's trash at me,
*Stuck up bitch.* I stopped drinking
when I realized I was fighting
for the vodka at the bottom of the hill
more than I was fighting against the terrible
things that could have happened to me
inside the cab of that rusty Chevy. I stopped drinking
before cell phones. I stopped drinking
after *Days of Wine and Roses.* I stopped drinking
even as I kept walking to El Prado Spirits
and the man behind the counter who recognized me
asked if I was alright. I didn't tell him
what had happened because he might have called
the police and then I would have had to wait
for them to arrive to fill out a report, delaying my Smirnoff.
I stopped drinking even before I had that last sip,
as I ran back up the hill squeezing a bottle by its neck.

# LISA

## Kera Bolonik

On April 11, 1995, exactly ten years ago, my friend Lisa fashioned a noose from a bathrobe belt, tied it to the bar of her hallway closet, looped the other end around her neck, and hung herself. When her fiancé found her, Lisa's toes were just grazing the floor—she was so determined to kill herself, she had summoned the strength to hold up her own feet. It was less than two weeks before her wedding.

For the next two days, the hospital kept Lisa on a respirator as they surveyed for brain activity, while fifteen to twenty members of her family and friends held vigil in the waiting area. I'll never forget what I saw when I went into her room in the intensive care unit: my friend's body lying still except for the rise and fall of her chest as air was pumped into her lungs; her eyes closed, a light magenta bruise encircling her neck. Her father wailed as he kneeled beside her. He'd been in that room all day, consumed by grief, hoping somehow she could miraculously pull through.

But when I looked at Lisa in that bed, I knew the next time I'd see her would be at her funeral. The following day, my funny, loving, dear friend of seven years was taken off the respirator, and she died. She was only twenty-four. The people who loved her were left to deal with the anguish, confusion and indignation at the absolute wrongness of the situation. I felt these things acutely and something else, too: terror. There had been many times when my own depression had made me feel desperate enough to contemplate suicide. But I'd always thought I could handle it and wait out the difficult periods. Lisa's suicide made me see things differently. She was my age, my size, a friend with whom I'd shared classes, books, albums, friends, jokes, values. I realized for the first time that there were two Lisas, and I'd known only one of them. The other Lisa was filled with rage and torment, and she had killed the friend I adored.

Ironic is too blithe a word to describe the tragic fact that Lisa had talked more people off the ledge during college than any crisis hotline, then went on to succeed in killing herself. I was one of those people, and I had survived while she had not.

I had coped with depression for half my life. Most of the time, I was extroverted, enthusiastic and optimistic. But from the age of twelve until Lisa's death, I had feelings of fury, melancholy and humiliation, and when they'd reach the boiling point, I'd secretly fantasize about suicide. When that mind-set took hold, I'd sleep all the time, then not at all. I was almost always paranoid, convinced everyone was making fun of me. I'd become obsessed with an especially cool group of people, and then I'd abruptly withdraw from them and the rest of my friends.

At first my mother dismissed my sullen moods as adolescent rebellion. But when at one point I suddenly spurned all of my friends and stayed up all night, every night, for over a week, she became concerned that something was seriously wrong with me. At fifteen, I was evaluated by a psychiatrist who diagnosed me with clinical depression and referred me to a psychotherapist. These were the years before antidepressants were dispensed like aspirin. So the doctor recommended counseling but didn't prescribe medication to stabilize the moods that had me swinging from hyperactive, yammering social butterfly to morose, fatalistic recluse.

Lisa was one of the first friends I made at my college, Rutgers University in New Brunswick, New Jersey, and she quickly became the one person I counted on when I'd get depressed. I'd often turn up at her door following one of my panicked, weepy evening phone calls, apologizing profusely. She'd invite me in, pour us each a mug of cheap jug wine, and stay up with me until the wee hours detangling the syntax in my English literature papers or parsing horrendous breakup and make-up conversations. Lisa was exceedingly patient with my repetitive, self-absorbed rants about how this professor must think I'm an idiot and that crush must think I'm a twit, assuring me that I wasn't stupid, that I was worthy. Her calm, easygoing manner was infectious, and eventually I would relax. And then she'd coax a smile from me by prompting me with some lyrics from Madonna's "Justify My Love," which we'd recite in our hammiest New York accents: "Tell me your dreams—am I in 'em? Tell me your fears—are ya scared?" Without fail, we'd both end up collapsing into paroxysms of laughter.

When I was alone, with the phone turned off and my roommates gone, however, I would imagine slitting my wrists with my X-Acto knife, climbing into a warm bath and drifting off into death. I found this fantasy soothing. Just knowing that I could put an end to my emotional torment calmed me down. I didn't yet realize that there was no such thing as a peaceful suicide. After graduating from college, I tried to treat my brief but chronic relapses into depression like the common cold. I'd call in sick, curl up in my bed, wait it out, and remind myself that no matter how miserable and hopeless I felt, in time I'd recover. Fortunately, after a few weeks, I always did.

I was in such a state the week before Lisa died. I'd taken time off from my publishing job and spent the entire week in my studio apartment, alone. The depression was fierce, more aggressive than I'd ever experienced. I told myself I had to find a psychiatrist who would prescribe Prozac or Zoloft, but I could barely get myself out of bed. After a week at home, I finally dragged myself into the office. That night, I came home to hear the message that Lisa was in intensive care in a New Jersey hospital.

I rode the first morning train out to New Brunswick. Suddenly, my depression struck me as self-indulgent and petty. Lisa had been suffering something terribly pernicious, more so than anything I'd experienced, but I never saw the signs. She wasn't a cutter, a bulimic, a hard drinker, a drug user, or a daredevil behind the wheel. She'd never tried suicide before the attempt that killed her. She had a supportive, loving family; a kind, devoted man who adored her; a good job as a high school English teacher. And Lisa had plans: After the wedding, she and her new husband were going to move from New Jersey to Brooklyn, and she would begin a master's program in education. I wasn't aware that she had a horrifying plan B.

I knew that Lisa had struggled with a bout of depression once during the previous year, but she had been successfully treated with medication and therapy. It was only after her death that I learned Lisa's illness had come back with a vengeance, eating away at her as voraciously and malignantly as a fast-growing tumor. She mustered all of her energy to function for her students and shut down when she got home. Lisa told her college roommate that when she revealed the intensity of her depression to her family and fiancé, they convinced her to take a leave of absence from her job. They even debated putting her in the hospital. But ultimately, she may have been too far gone.

In my last conversation with Lisa, we spoke for over an hour about her wedding, graduate school, plans to move to my neighborhood—and her past battle with depression. When she'd talked about it before, it was with a certain confident detachment. This time, Lisa sounded rattled. "It was really scary," she said. "But things are much more manageable now." Her voice returned to normal over the course of the conversation, so I believed her. I asked if she and her fiancé were planning to start a family. "No," she said, abruptly, as if to say, it's not up for discussion, my mind's never going to change. Throughout the phone call, I found myself reflexively expressing every loving sentiment I'd ever wanted to share with her. I told her she'd taught me what it meant to be a friend. At the time, I thought I was just getting emotional in anticipation of her wedding. Later, I would recall this conversation with a mixture of horror and relief, wondering, in retrospect, if I unconsciously sensed something beneath her surface composure.

Lisa's suicide literally scared the life into me: Lying in that hospital bed, she showed me the awful difference between fantasizing about suicide and actually following through. To this day, whenever a suicidal thought creeps into my mind, I only need to refer back to that image of Lisa on a respirator to remind myself of what it really means to do it. At the same time, I recognized my own vulnerability; I hadn't given depression enough credit. It was deceptive, acting like a mere nuisance as it sabotaged my work, my friendships, my love life. And my depressed periods were getting worse with age, each battle more wearing than the last. I realized I had to arm myself if I wanted to continue to win.

I found myself a psychotherapist, whom I saw every week for nearly ten years. The first year, we talked about what brought me into her office—my grief about Lisa, my fears of suicidal thoughts. As difficult as therapy was, I went back every week—I needed it. And I sensed that it was effective, because I started to approach my life differently. I liked how therapy changed me.

I was also referred to a psychopharmacologist who prescribed Prozac, Paxil and Celexa, but each drug made me anxious, asexual, overweight and unable to cry. Then we landed on my perfect cocktail—Wellbutrin and Topamax. I got back my libido, my metabolism, and best of all, my emotional life. Over time, I started to feel more relaxed and confident. I've had setbacks—last year I took a work problem to heart and had a harder time getting things done for nearly two months—but even at my worst, I've been able to get myself out of bed before 7 A.M. and slog through my inbox. And four years ago, I began my first healthy relationship with someone who doesn't inspire 2 A.M. weep-fests. I know Lisa would have approved of my partner, and I'm devastated they'll never meet.

I still think about Lisa every day. There are times when I'm watching a movie, and I'll remember having first seen it with her. Or I'll become obsessed with a new band and imagine that Lisa would've shared my passion for them. There are whole days when I have to remind myself that her suicide even happened in the first place. They usually follow the nights when I've had a dream about her; it's the same dream every time. We are having a picnic, and I ask her how long she is visiting, a question she never answers. The words tumble out of my mouth before I can stop them: I tell her how devastating it was. The hospital. The funeral. Her parents' unending sorrow. I'm sorry I'm telling you all this, I say in my dream. She takes my hand in hers, looks at me sympathetically and smiles gently, as though we're talking about someone else. I'm reminded of the Lisa I loved so much, and I wake up with a catch in my throat, missing her even more.

# THE DOPPLER EFFECT

## B.H. Fairchild

When I would go into bars in those days
the hard round faces would turn
to speak something like loneliness
but deeper, the rain spilling into gutters
or the sound of a car pulling away
in a moment of sleeplessness just before dawn,
the Doppler effect, I would have said shrewdly then,
of faces diminishing slightly into the distance
even as they spoke. Their children
were doing well, somewhere, and their wives
were somewhere, too, and we were here
with those bright euphoric flowers
unfolding slowly in our eyes
and the sun which we had not seen for days
nuzzling our fingertips and licking
our elbows. Oh, it was all there,
and there again the same, our heads nodding,
hands resting lightly upon the mahogany sheen
of the bar. Then one of us would leave
and the door would turn to a yellow square
so sudden and full of fire
that our eyes would daze and we would
stare into the long mirrors for hours
and speak shrewdly of that pulling away,
that going toward something.

# THRALL

## Frederick and Steven Barthelme

*A few weeks before Thanksgiving 1996, Frederick and Steven Barthelme were escorted away from the blackjack tables at a Mississippi casino. Within a year, the brothers faced criminal charges for allegedly cheating with the help of the dealer. Though the Barthelmes were both respected authors and college professors, they suddenly found themselves reeling from the consequences of their shared addiction to gambling. The brothers were eventually cleared of the charges and restored their reputations, but they never regained the $250,000 they lost over a three-year period. In their memoir,* Double Down, *the Barthelmes describe their descent into the gripping world of slot machines and blackjack tables.*

We had heard about gambling and addiction, about people who had lost their jobs, their houses, their cars, their families, their lives. We'd heard about people who got crosswise with a bookie or other unconventional lender. We had seen the gambling movies, Karel Reisz's *The Gambler*, Robert Altman's *California Split*. We had read Dostoyevsky's novella. We had read *Under the Volcano*, seen *The Lost Weekend* and *Days of Wine and Roses*. We wondered if that was us. Decided that it was.

We discussed addiction on those long drives down Highway 49. We were analytical about it, examined it in excruciating detail. We knew that your average psychologist would have said we were addicts in a minute. We knew the threatening jargon, that we were "enabling" each other, that we were a codependency case, and in the normal course of things, had we seen ourselves flying to the coast every four or five days for eighteen hours of blackjack and slot machines, we might have said we were addicts. But in the car headed down there this characterization seemed insufficient.

There was a catch: So what? Being an addict didn't mean anything. One of the virtues of having gambling as your vice—as opposed to sex, drugs, or alcohol—was that the disadvantages were felt only at the bank. As long as you had the bankroll, these disadvantages were only before the wounds amounted to much, and the customary assumption (which all of the movies, books, and hand-wringing newspaper articles made) that the later, catastrophic stages were inevitable was something we didn't buy. We doubted it. We had been trained to doubt the omnipotent sway of psychology.

Ours was not a family brought up on psychology. In our father's view, the great seething life of feelings could be a damn nuisance. Father had more than a teaspoon of the Frank Bunker Gilbreth about him. Although the family did recognize the psychological dimension, pragmatism—some kind of physical pragmatism—superseded psychology when explanations or remedies were wanted.

Being good sons of our father, we rode to the coast night after night, streaming through the sweltering Mississippi heat, clouds of grasshoppers popping off the highway like a plague of sparks, humidity as thick as gravy, and when we said to each other that we were addicts, when we talked about being addicts, it was a joke—a joke with a nasty twist, but still a joke. Later, after we became accused felons we would call each other Lyle and Erik, with the idea that a joke needs a Menendezian edge.

You're a gambling addict, so what? Have you got money in the bank? Yes? Go on being an addict. A part of the pleasure was being able to go over the top, way over the top, without any of the mess or travail associated with doing drugs or becoming alcoholics or cheating on our wives, which is not to say the wives approved. They did not. But neither did they react the way they might have had we become enmeshed in other vices.

Sometimes, at first, they went with us. Later, not. But even then, during our long gambling nights, we would call in, advise our spouses how we were doing, how far ahead or behind we were, tell them that we loved them. And we did love them, somehow more fiercely when we were at the coast, when we were free to go to the coast. Something about the intensity of the experience of gambling, of risking the money, of risking loss, made the security and solidity of the home front much more important, much more sweet. More than that, it was a detachment, the anesthetic clarity with which you sometimes saw things in the middle of a drunk. Once Rick stood at the bank of telephones downstairs at the Grand, leaning his forehead against the chrome surface of a wall phone, standing there after hanging up from a conversation with Rie. They had exchanged *I love yous* and suddenly, after the call, he felt that love with crippling intensity.

An addict is someone who "surrenders" to something, the dictionary will tell you, "habitually or obsessively." Most people are at least a little addicted to something— work, food, exercise, sex, watching sports on television, cooking, reading, the stock market. Some people are addicted to washing their hands. Some people trim their hedges from dawn to dusk. Some people play too much golf. Almost anything can be the object of addiction.

Whatever his pleasure, an addict usually knows he is, or may be, an addict, but inside the warmth of his addiction, the label seems secondary, does not signify, as we like to say over at the college. It's like telling a horse he's a horse. Take President Clinton, for example. When he was involved in certain activities, he must have known he was addicted to something; he just didn't care. We felt just like the president. We didn't care. We supposed, in our conversations, both in Hattiesburg and en route to the coast, that when the time came we would bail. We knew that push would come to shove at some point, and at that point we would get out of the game.

Steve, wisely but very late in all this, bought a house with some of his inheritance. Made a down payment, got a low mortgage, invested in a home. Buying houses didn't come easy to us, in part because the house in which we had grown up was as much a cultural declaration as a dwelling, embodying ideas about design always to be defended against Philistines. Since we had left that house, we had lived in more or less ordinary houses for many years, but we had always rented. Buying an undistinguished house seemed like giving in, disloyalty. There were other reasons, of course. We had led unstable lives, so the idea of settling in the same place for thirty years had seemed laughable. Until Steve started teaching, and for some time afterward, he had never had the steady income to envision buying a house. Buying a house seemed rash when half one's worldly goods were in cardboard boxes awaiting the next move.

We admitted to having "addictive personalities," but we liked our addiction, the object of our addiction. It wasn't so different from all the other things, large and small, that we had intense attachments to—Diet Coke and Russian writers, springer spaniels and computers, box wrenches and movies. From childhood we had been taught that the object of an addiction was secondary. It was the way in which you cared about something, the quality of your interest rather than its object, that mattered. The first measure of the quality of an interest was its intensity, its thoroughgoingness. Best was to surrender oneself to something habitually or obsessively. We had done that all our lives.

Now the important thing was gambling. The care and feeding of our addiction, the pleasure of our addiction. Gambling was a very cerebral, almost slow-motion activity, which made it easy to savor. It was markedly more satisfying because we were doing it together. As brothers, we shared all the surprise and exhilaration of a new and consuming interest, like any new hobby—skydiving, methamphetamine. Codependency has its good side. Both doing it, we were each part performer and part audience. Every gambling session wrote its own swift, strange story, filled with highs and lows, finely calibrated details ("she flipped another five...") and compelling nuances ("and I thought, 'Fuck, ace, next one's an ace,' and then sure as shit..."). Gamblers want to talk. For us, there was always someone to tell, someone who knew in his blood what you were talking about. After a trip, our conversations went on for days, full of lurid, taunting laughter. The kind that revealed just how completely we were hooked on risk, on gambling.

We weren't measuring ourselves against the real daredevils of the culture; we were measuring ourselves against other normal people, middle-class people, good solid stock, people with jobs, families, houses, cars, and responsibilities that they dispatched in a workmanlike way. People like us. We told ourselves that betting a thousand dollars on a hand of blackjack might be stupid, but it wasn't as stupid as shooting yourself full of heroin, or as various members of our family had done for years, drinking yourself into oblivion by five o'clock in the afternoon—or better yet, doing it by noon, waking up at three and doing it again by five, having dinner and doing it again by nine. Maybe we were just looking for a way to keep up with the rest of the family, members of which had had their troubles with various forms of conspicuous consumption, of obsession, of well, for lack of a better word, addiction. Yes, it ran in the family. From our father on down, maybe even from *his* father on down.

The only time you really think of yourself as an addict is when you want to stop. When it's time to stop. When you're in so much trouble that stopping is the only thing left. But we never got there. We could afford it. It was fun. It was a way to blow off steam. It took us out of ourselves in a way that we hadn't been taken out of ourselves by anything else.

We had had good luck with addictions in the past. Both of us had been drinkers and smokers. Rick had been a drunk in his early twenties, but had stopped dead after he moved to New York and discovered that getting drunk and waking up at four A.M. on a Lower East Side street was not healthy. Steve had long since given up heavy drinking for steady drinking, three drinks a day, give or take a couple, for the past thirty years. Both of us had had smoking habits—two or three packs a day—and while we'd tried to curb them, following the path of declining tar and nicotine, going from regular cigarettes to pretend cigarettes like True and Carlton, we'd had no intention of quitting until, as mentioned, our two older brothers were diagnosed with throat cancer one within a month of the other.

We quit smoking.

But gambling wasn't producing a downside for us. Gambling was only producing the release, the euphoria, and the opportunity to behave bizarrely, just like—we imagined—ordinary, everyday people. We didn't think we were wild and crazy; we thought gambling made us regular guys.

It was an aesthetic thing too. Everywhere around us were writers and artists and professors, hard at work at what Ishmael Reed describes as "all wearing the same funny hat." It had long seemed obvious that the best course was the other direction. Neither of us had the customary late-twentieth-century middle-class phobia for people who were deemed ordinary. In fact, ordinary was what we both liked best.

What we didn't like about the academy was the falseness: conservative people presenting themselves in Che Guevara suits, digging hard for career advantage while settling hearty congratulations all around for assigning radical authors to their students to read, thus threatening the established order. Soon they would take their SUVs into the mountains.

This put a little extra heat under the affection we had for the ordinary people we imagined existed somewhere and for whom we felt a special kinship. It was ordinariness that we were extending with our gambling, by being addicted to it, by doing it to excess, by risking more money than made any sense at all, by telling ourselves that we were going to win, or that we might win, when we knew as surely as anybody else that the likelihood of that was slim. Still, you'd be surprised at how much positive thinking goes on, on the highway at midnight.

You'd be surprised by how dearly the heart holds the idea that tonight you might actually win, that this two thousand dollars, the last two thousand you have in your bank account, will be the basis of your big comeback. Even in the heat of battle, down five or fifteen thousand in a night, the not particularly well-heeled but still liquid blackjack loser can imagine winning it all back in a flash.

And he would not imagine it had he not already done it once or twice or maybe more. Had he not experienced that thrill of the cards having run against him all night, run against him for five consecutive hours and having in that time lost an enormous amount of money, gone to the cashier's cage again and again, new resources, the thrill that comes when the cards turn, when they become your cards, when they became his cards, not the casino's, when in the space of forty-five minutes you recognize that you're going to win whatever you bet. And if you recognize it soon enough, and if you're secure enough in the recognition, you can turn around the whole night, turn around five thousand dollars in twenty minutes. You can turn around fifteen thousand dollars in an hour.

It's a rare, even amazing experience. It almost makes gambling worthwhile. Everything you touch turns to gold. You bet five hundred dollars and you bet a thousand. You double down and win. Your stacks of chips grow. Pretty soon they are paying you in hundreds, then five hundreds— the purple chips. You've got a stack of those in front of you.

Then, if the going is really good, they start paying you in orange—the thousand-dollar chips. The thousand-dollar chips are slightly larger, a sixteenth of an inch larger in diameter than all the other chips. You stack them separately.

Your stack grows, and maybe you bet one of them or two of them on a hand. Or you play two hands. And still you win. Sure, this isn't Monte Carlo, you're not some duke or some heiress, and so you're not betting hundreds of thousands of dollars a hand, but that fact makes your betting and your winning just that much sweeter, because you have no business in the world betting a thousand dollars on a hand of blackjack, and you know it. So when you do, and when the cards are coming your way, and when your five thousand turns to ten, your ten to twenty, it's mesmerizing. Suddenly that business they always say about feeling like you'll live forever becomes a little bit true, because you've crossed over some line, gone into some other territory, become somebody else.

You're part of the table, part of the machine that plays blackjack, part of the casino, part of the system. Only you're not the part that gives your money to them anymore, you're not the part you usually play: the mark, the bozo. You've skidded out onto the ice in the middle of the Olympics in a huge stadium filled with cheering people and swaying, lime-colored spotlights and, suddenly, inexplicably, you can skate like an angel.

# PUTTING DOWN THE DUCK

## Margaret Bullitt-Jonas

Many years after I stopped eating compulsively, long after I walked into my first meeting of Overeaters Anonymous, at once anxious and hopeful, wary and eager, with my eyes downcast, my heart pounding with anxiety, and my coat wrapped tightly around my bulging body (having gained twenty pounds in the past six weeks), I happened to see a clip from *Sesame Street* that made me burst out laughing. As I remember the sequence, Ernie is clutching his beloved rubber ducky when he comes upon a jazz band. Suddenly there's nothing that Ernie wants to do more than to play jazz too. He wants to join in, catch the rhythm and carry the beat, add his own distinctive voice to the cascading play of sound. He wants to pick up the saxophone and let his spirit soar. But there's just one little problem: his hands are already full. He can't play the saxophone if he's clinging to his duck. What should he do? Ernie is worried and confused, torn between conflicting desires.

At last, an unlikely assortment of advisors steps forward to release him from his dilemma. To the brisk and jazzy beat of the band, this improbable collection of newscasters, actors, musicians, and performers—including, among others, Harry Reasoner, Barbara Walters, Itzhak Perlman, Paul Simon, Ralph Nader, and some of the stars of *Taxi* and *Upstairs Downstairs*—repeats one after the other the same, very simple advice: "Put down the ducky. Put down the ducky. You've got to put down the ducky if you want to play the saxophone." Their voices are sometimes chiding and sometimes kind, sometimes coaxing and sometimes stern, sometimes melodic and sometimes tuneless, but their message is always the same: if you want to make music, you have to let go of the ducky.

Why did I laugh? Because it's so obvious: no one can play the saxophone and hold a rubber ducky at the same time. Because I saw myself in Ernie: like him, I longed, when I came in to OA [Overeaters Anonymous], to join with life, to let loose, to let my spirit fly free. And because, like him, I was afraid. I needed encouragement to do what was so obvious and yet so terrifyingly difficult, so simple and yet so terribly hard: to put down the food and live.

My early weeks and months in OA revolved around one simple message, one basic refrain that began to pulse through my mind with the regularity of a heartbeat: Don't eat, no matter what. No matter what, don't eat.

In the lexicon of OA, the verb "to eat" when it stands alone without a direct object, is shorthand for "compulsive overeating." To refuse "to eat" means to refuse the first compulsive bite, to refuse to binge. If I wanted to have a life, if I wanted to find out who I was and why I was here on this earth, if I wanted to learn how to love and how to let love in, if I wanted to be happy and at peace with myself, if I wanted my existence to have any sense of meaning or purpose, if I wanted nothing more noble or ambitious than simply to stop being so miserable and so filled with self-hatred—if I wanted *any* of these things, I'd have to stop eating compulsively. I'd have to put the food down. It was as stark, as simple, and as scary as that.

Addiction is now widely considered to be a threefold illness, at once physical, emotional, and spiritual. To some degree, our healing takes place on all three levels at once, but in the early stages of recovery, the addict must focus all her energy and attention on physical recovery. The enormous challenge in my first weeks of OA was unambiguous and unequivocal: not to overeat, no matter what. As far as physical recovery is concerned, it makes no difference what you're feeling. It doesn't matter if you're angry with your mother and don't know what to say. It doesn't matter if your boyfriend has left you, if your cat has died, or if you've just bounced your rent check. It doesn't matter if you think nobody loves you, if there's half an hour to kill before the plane takes off and you're worried about the flight, if you've blown or aced the exam, if your boss just chewed you out or handed you a bonus. It doesn't matter if you just found out you're pregnant, or if you just found out you're not. It doesn't matter if you're stressed out, bored, or lonely, if you're angry or ecstatic, sorrowful or joyful, excited or exhausted. In fact, it doesn't matter *what* you're feeling, or what's going on, or not going on, in your life. In any case, in every case, the same principle holds true: you don't eat, no matter what. No matter what, you don't eat.

Physical recovery isn't about nuances of feelings or insights into why you overeat. It's simply about behavior, about what a person does or doesn't do. Did the hand reach for the fork, the spoon, the extra food, or not? Was the lid screwed back on the jar of peanut butter, or not? Was the cereal box closed after one serving was taken, or not? Was the piece of cake refused, or not? For someone like me, long accustomed to handling every problem, challenge, and feeling by eating over it, this was a radical reorientation indeed. Day after day, the OA program asked me to accept the fact that although excessive food had once served me as lover and friend, companion and confidante, those days were over. For good. A line had been crossed. An activity that had once given me some measure of solace and satisfaction now brought nothing but misery. Food was no longer the answer. The answer was not in the food. Like every other addict, I had to put the rubber ducky down if I wanted to make any music with my life.

I needed to hear this message over and over again. In the first months of recovery, I needed to hear it every day, and many times a day, because it so easily slipped out of awareness. Left to my own devices, I could easily fall back into the familiar cacophony of voices that always preceded a binge. What was one little bite after all? How bad could one little slip be? What was the big deal? Who would care, who would know, if I just helped myself to a few extra slices of bread, had just another spoonful or two of peanut butter? How bad could a few bites be? I could always go back to OA the next day and begin again—right?

I remember having lunch with an OA friend just one week after I'd come into OA, one week after I'd begun eating with moderation and care. I remember casually remarking that I was thinking about going on a binge that night. My friend lunged across the table, grabbed my elbows, and looked me squarely in the eye.

"Focus!" she cried. "Focus! You need to make two phone calls. You need to get to another meeting today." And then came the refrain that had slipped my mind, the refrain that cut through all the wheedling, seductive voices spinning webs of confusion within my head: "Just don't eat. Whatever else you do today, just don't eat. A good day is a day in which you don't eat compulsively. Even if you accomplish nothing else today—even if you don't do a stitch of work, even if you're a bitch all day, even if you lie around all day in your pajamas—if you don't eat, it's a good day. Just get through today without eating. That's all you have to do. Eat tomorrow, if you have to. But don't eat today."

My friend's fervor shocked me to my senses. I was startled that somebody cared so much about whether or not I self-destructed with food. Jarred awake by her clarity, I remembered who I was: a compulsive eater trying to recover, one day at a time. And I remembered, too, the insidious nature of an eating disorder: an extra bite here or there might not matter in itself, but before long an extra bite could swell into an extra serving, and then, like a sleep-walker wandering through her own private nightmare, within a few days I could be polishing off all the food in the house. In the wink of an eye I could find myself sliding back down into the chaos that had so recently been killing me.

So I did what she told me, what I now knew I *must* do if I wanted to save my life. I got myself to another meeting. I made two phone calls. I put together another day of abstinence.

It is friends like that, support like that, that empowers the powerless. It is friends like that, support like that, that carries each recovering person through another day of sobriety or another day of abstinence, until the days gradually become weeks, and the weeks, years. That incident over lunch was just one critical moment among many when my OA friends prodded me to pay attention and stay awake, giving me the strength to listen and stay faithful to my own deep desire for healing. On the days when I lost my desire to stay well, when I could find no motivation not to overeat and plenty of reasons why I should, my OA friends encouraged me to stay abstinent anyway, until I could again claim for myself the longing to be whole and to be set free. In the meantime, until that moment came, they would carry my heart's desire for me. Physical recovery came first, even if desire and insight lagged temporarily behind.

Just as my life had once revolved around food, so too did the early stages of recovery revolve around abstinence. Eating in moderation—what OA calls abstinence—had to become the central focus of each day, for it was the task that made any other task possible. Every morning I had to ask myself: What do I need to do today in order to maintain my abstinence? What must I do to keep food in its rightful place?

I remember being taken aback, in my early days in the program, by an insistent and solemn refrain that played through our meetings like a recurring motif: "Abstinence is the most important thing in my life without exception."

"Jeepers," I sputtered to myself. "What about your spouse, your family, your friends? What about world peace? Or social justice? What about God?"

Only after some experience with the program did I come to see that for a compulsive overeater, maintaining abstinence is like focusing a camera: if the image in the center is clear, the whole picture comes into focus. Only if my food is clear am I free to love self, family, and friends. Only if I'm abstinent am I free to give myself to larger goals, or to God.

In order to help keep that clarity at the center, the OA program offers a variety of tools. In order to maintain my abstinence, I learned I must use them all. For instance, I learned to go to meetings. In the first months of recovery, I went to at least one meeting a day. In church basements and hospital cafeterias, in classrooms and meeting rooms, in corridors and halls, I met with strangers from all walks of life who were somehow just like me in the ways that mattered—people whose struggles and conflicts, shames and fears, desires and hopes, I could recognize as variations of my own. Here was a resting place for me, a place to find welcome and acceptance, a place to tell the truth. Here was a place to gain inspiration and hope, a community in whose company I could begin the slow process of healing, even though in the early days I felt too shy to speak and could do nothing more than watch and listen.

In meetings I found a world quite distinct from the world of my family—a world in which I could take my first faltering steps toward telling the truth, making my pain explicit, taking responsibility for my choices, and slowly setting aside blame. I didn't know it then, but the more I saturated myself in twelve-step meetings, the more I was learning a whole new way of life, one that empowered me not only to stop eating compulsively, but also to find new ways of relating to myself and to my family. Twelve-step meetings can change you. When you reenter your family, step back into the fray, you're no longer the same person.

I learned to use another tool of the twelve-step program: I found a sponsor, a person who had more experience in recovery than I did and was willing to offer me personal guidance as I groped my way toward wholeness.

I learned to commit myself to a daily food plan. I learned to avoid binge foods and sugar. I learned to take time to plan and to fix in writing what I intended to eat each day.

I learned to "turn over" my food to my sponsor, to "give my food plan away." For all my embarrassment at sharing such an intimate part of my life with somebody else, I learned to call my sponsor every morning and tell her what I planned to eat.

I learned to make other phone calls too. Addiction is rightly considered a disease of isolation. When loneliness closed in, when I felt anxious or overwhelmed, agitated or upset, I learned to pick up the phone instead of diving into the food. I learned to ask for help. I learned to carry a little notebook with me, which I slowly filled with OA members' phone numbers and first names. I learned, despite my shame and anxiety, that it was in fact possible to call someone I barely knew, possible to ask for a few minutes of someone's time, possible to talk about what was "eating" me until the urge to eat had passed.

I learned that it was possible to be abstinent if I took each day one by one; if I chose to live, as the program puts it, "one day at a time." The thought of giving up sugar forever was intolerable. The thought of a lifetime without Halloween candy, Thanksgiving pie, Christmas cookies, Valentine's Day chocolate, or cake and ice cream on my birthday, was more than I could bear. Just thinking about this loss was enough to evoke such anxiety and self-pity that I was tempted to plunge headlong into a binge. So I learned not to dwell on words like "never," "always," and "forever." Maybe one day I would eat sugar again, I told myself, but just for today I needed to protect my abstinence. I learned to focus on what I must do to stay abstinent just for now, just for today. If a twenty-four-hour stretch of abstinence seemed too long to endure, I focused on what I must do to stay abstinent for the next hour, or the next five minutes.

At various points in my recovery, I brought my own food with me to wedding receptions and on airplane flights. I weighed and measured my food, both alone at home and with others in restaurants. Sometimes I ate with chopsticks. Their awkwardness made me eat more slowly, tasting every bite. In the intense first weeks of the program, when my body was enduring some analogue of a drunk's going through detox, my mind topsy-turvy with the stress of withdrawal, I needed to simplify my life—to cancel unnecessary appointments, refuse dinner engagements, turn down projects—so that I could focus all my energy on the challenge before me: to eat with awareness, to eat with care.

For a long time, "working the program" meant being willing to look weird. I remember a friend of mine watching with bemusement as we prepared lunch one day at my house shortly after I joined OA. She wasn't one of my handful of "eating friends." She was one of the friends who thought I was fairly normal around food, someone who hardly gave my eating habits a second thought. In her presence, I'd always eaten sensibly, waiting until I was alone before pulling out all the stops and gorging on whatever I could find. I'd already planned what I would say if she or anyone else ever commented about my having gained some weight. I'd shrug and look perplexed, as if she had presented me with a mystery that I myself didn't understand, as if I had no idea how it could have happened, it must have been something in the air I breathed.

Now that I was abstinent, I handled food in public the same way that I handled it in private. A day at a time, the ancient deadly split between my secret self and the self I showed the world was being mended. I was done with lying about food. So in front of my astonished friend I did exactly what I did when I prepared an abstinent meal alone. I pulled out a measuring cup. I stuffed as much cooked broccoli into the cup as it could possibly hold. I pressed that broccoli down. I mashed it into shapeless pulp. I squeezed in every bit of green leaf and fiber, until the measuring cup was packed to the brim. Then I took a knife and slid it carefully across the top.

My friend raised her eyebrows quizzically. "Is *this* what recovery is all about?" she asked.

How fussy this was, she seemed to imply, how patently greedy. Of course she was right. And I was stricken with shame (Now she knows how greedy I really am! How strange I am around food!) Yet even in those early weeks in OA, I knew that I had been given the tools—the map, the compass—that could lead me out of the woods. But only if I was willing to use them and put up with looking like a fool. Only if I could face my shame and not let it stop me.

I explained my new routine to my friend. I'm sure I was defensive. I couldn't help but be embarrassed, but there it was; this was what I needed to do, if I was going to save my life. I'd "committed" my food for the day, I told her. I'd promised my sponsor I'd eat a cup of broccoli as part of my lunch, and so one cup I'd have, no more and no less. I was entitled to a full cup of broccoli, and I didn't want to feel deprived. When it came to food, I told my friend, I needed total clarity. For now, at least, I couldn't trust my eyes to tell me what "one serving" of broccoli might be. For me, eating "one serving" of anything meant eating the whole thing, entire, all at once. Something external and objective—a measuring cup, a teaspoon, a portable scale—could let me know where the limits lay. Then I'd be free to taste and to enjoy my food. And I'd know that it was safe, that it wasn't more than my body needed, that it wouldn't lead me to binge.

Was all of this rigid? Without a doubt. Was it obsessive? Certainly. Was it necessary? I'm convinced of it. Like a house whose foundation has eroded and whose walls are toppling, I needed to be braced by an external scaffolding that could hold and contain me while the basic repairs were being made. All the insights and good intentions in the world weren't enough to stop my addictive behavior. Food had a way of slipping into my mouth even before I'd made any sort of conscious choice. Somehow the spoon was licked clean, the extra helpings were grabbed, the hand was already in motion toward the mouth, before I knew it or clearly intended it. I needed a structure outside me to help me stop—guidelines to follow, a path to walk, a net to catch me when I slipped.

More than fifteen years have passed since I came into OA, and how I work the program has changed radically. I no longer need a scaffolding to surround me so closely. There's room now for some flexibility and spontaneity when it comes to food, although I still never touch sugar. I figure it's best to let sleeping dogs lie. No more battles with Cerberus at the gates of hell. I never want to tackle that beast again.

I no longer go to many meetings, no longer follow the guidance of a sponsor or turn over a daily food plan. I no longer weigh and measure food before it goes into my mouth or travel with a measuring cup and scale. And no, I don't mash my broccoli into a pulp anymore. I eat three moderate meals a day and keep second helpings and snacks to a minimum.

Do I have to stay alert with food? Absolutely. Am I still a compulsive overeater? Yes, although a day at a time I live in balance, in grateful recovery. Am I anxious about food, worried about my weight, absorbed in the struggle to make peace with what I do or do not eat? No. The tools of OA have done their good work. The house is standing. Its windows are open wide to the world. Its doors are able to open and close. The walls of the self are durable again: there are clearer boundaries to me now, an outside and an inside, the capacity to say yes and the capacity to say no. I can eat with pleasure when I'm hungry and stop eating when I'm full.

And yet, although I don't use the OA tools as I once did, I still know they're nearby whenever I need them. If the roof springs a leak or a wall begins to sag, if food begins to call me again with its siren song, to lure me with its phony promises and deceptive deals, I know what to do and where to go. I pick up the tools at once. I get on the phone and talk with an OA friend. Recommit myself to abstinence. Pray. Write. Ask for help. If need be, I go to a meeting.

But the first step in the long process of recovery, and the foundation of a food addict's subsequent well-being, is putting down the fork, putting down the food, one day at a time. No insight into self, however subtle; no analysis of the dynamics of addiction, however accurate; no understanding of the nature of desire, however sophisticated or enlightening—none of these fine things can substitute for action. The healing of addiction depends, first and foremost, not on what we know, nor on what we feel, but on what we do—a fact that remains as stubbornly true for "old-timers" as it does for newcomers.

After spending a certain amount of time in twelve-step meetings, almost anyone can master the language. We may learn to speak eloquently about the value of "surrender to a Higher Power." We may be able to rattle off glibly the tools of the program and explain their use. We may grasp the fine points of the *Big Book of Alcoholics Anonymous*, the basic text of all twelve-step programs. And yet if we take no action, if we don't use the tools about which we speak, if we don't put into practice the principles that we espouse, then full recovery will remain elusive.

When it comes to addiction, it's easy to kid ourselves and to settle for talk. That's why I learned in OA to mistrust so-called fat serenity, the pipe dream of being spiritually healthy and at peace, even though we continue to overeat as compulsively and chaotically as ever. OA taught me that physical recovery must come first. Action gives birth to insight. It's only when we put the food down that a deeper level of healing can arise; only when we stop our restless, random, greedy munching that we can begin to listen to the desire of our heart and to learn anything about what serenity might really be.

# TO DETTNER (my grandmother)

## Diana M. Raab

You took your life in the house where

we lived together forty years ago.
I was ten and you sixty.

Your ashen face and blonde bob
disheveled upon white sheets

on the stretcher held by paramedics
lightly grasping each end, and tiptoeing

down the creaking wooden stairs
you walked up the night before.

But now your body descends to the ambulance
and sirens swarm like vultures

around the place I once called home.
I wonder why you left in such a way,

as the depression gnawed
at your gentle heart, which cared for me

since my very first push into the world.
I've learned from you

never to give up, but to find
a passion and thank you

I did
I live to write

so I shall never die.

# SWEET ROLLS AND VODKA

## Victoria Patterson

### 1990

You are living with your grandparents at the age of twenty because you have been kicked out of a recovery home for women alcoholics. You had been residing at New Directions for Women after a twenty-eight-day stint for chemical dependency and depression in a psychiatric hospital. ("Sometimes all a woman needs in life is a new direction," says the pamphlet. The young woman in the photograph on the cover is seen walking briskly along the Back Bay in Costa Mesa, California. What the pamphlet doesn't mention is that later, after claiming to be a bisexual, she will relapse on pain pills due to a supposed back injury and move to Texas.)

Unable to shake habits of defiance, you had stayed out all night (curfew nine p.m.) with a member of the opposite sex, albeit a sober one with a big motorcycle he called his "hog," the wind whistling past your ears as he drove you helmet-less through the dark hills of Laguna Canyon. As you climbed through your recovery home window, sun rising, you knew the gig was up, and a note waited on your untouched pillow: This was your final warning. Pack today.

Even though you are sober and have recently taken a ninety-day plastic chip as proof (legend has it that a local bar accepts chips as payment for drinks), you feel like a failure: a college dropout, lush, and groupie. Life seems like an exhausting challenge, and your goals have become as simple as brushing your teeth and making your bed. You carry the chip with you in your pocket while you sell curled heaps of pastel-colored frozen yogurt at work. Meanwhile, your brother and friends are finishing college and embarking on respectable careers.

Your grandmother has offered her home, saying, "Stay here as long as you need." Your grandfather built the house on the bay in Corona del Mar the same year you were born. Your grandparents' home has always signified permanence and stability. The proposal sinks into your core, makes you feel loved unconditionally, and binds you to them permanently, which is ironic since they are the hard asses of the family—judgmental, powerful, wealthy—and you understand your rebellion to be in large part inspired by your grandfather. You had self-righteously accused him during "family therapy" of being at the heart of your family's dysfunction. (He was stoned on martinis at the time, and it was testimony to his love for you that he came to the session at all.)

Family members treat your grandparents with reverence and fear. Even your mother expresses jealousy that your grandparents do not disown you. Your grandparents' inclusion has given you a strange, exalting power, and you feel safe and loved within the warm comfort of their home. (Literally warm, since your grandfather heats the house to seventy-eight degrees.) They support you, expressing admiration, partially born from their mutual admitted alcoholism (only to you), and their inability and/or unwillingness to cease drinking.

It's a bewildering alliance, your alcoholism linked with theirs. At first you leave recovery pamphlets and literature on the bedside table where your grandfather naps. He leaves hints: a corner folded to mark his place; a pamphlet moved a different angle. Your hyper-recovery enthusiasm settles to a resigned hope, and a resolution to stick by them as they have done with you.

## 1991

A mournful noise, like a shriek and a howl combined, wakes you. One of your grandfather's golf clubs leans against the wall. Although you intuitively deem the noise not to be burglary or violence, you grab the club anyway, clutching the handle as you pad down the hallway, your bare feet sinking into the white carpet.

The silhouette of a man appears from around the corner, and you jump back. It's your grandfather. Seeing him in his striped boxers, with his slightly bowed, skinny legs, alarms you. He looks ridiculous and vulnerable, nothing like the imposing, mythic man you were trained as a child to "keep quiet" around.

He gasps. "Jesus Christ," he says. "Put my goddamn seven iron down." He runs a hand over his bald head. The strange howling continues.

"What is that?" you ask, resting the golf club against the wall.

"Cats screwing," he says, and his eyes light up wickedly, but then he looks embarrassed.

"Oh," you say, smiling. You look at his feet, which appear delicate, narrow and pale, the toes curved inward, a tan line at the base of his ankles where his golf socks end.

He stands on the patio and throws golf balls at the cats. "So we can get some peace, and some goddamn sleep," he says. The animals are on a ledge. The balls thump against the brick wall like small white bombs. Shadows rustle and leap. A breeze and a dark mass whisks past your legs.

"Jesus Christ," he says. "Did you feel that?" The two of you go back inside, and he shuts the sliding glass door. "Well, well, well," he says. You can tell he's enjoying himself. You kiss him good night, your fingers touching his forearm, lips brushing his stubble. He smells of vodka and toothpaste.

"G'night, honey," he says, in a sweet voice he reserves especially for you. He calls you "honey" often these days. Both your grandparents, never keen on displays of affection, have become increasingly demonstrative. Your grandmother likes to kiss you wetly on the lips, making a loud smacking noise and leaving coral lip prints and the lingering odor of Chanel No. 5.

You lie in bed surrounded by the smells of your grandparents and imagine them asleep in the next room. Waves shush-shush against the shore of the bay. A sense of calm overcomes you, as if you can rest for the first time in years. You fall asleep and dream of the bay water: steely black at night, mossy green in the day. Sometimes you are flying, arms spread, fingers skimming the surface, and when you look down into the water, the dark forms of stingrays lurk on the sandy bottom.

## 1998

You are staying at your grandparents' house just this one night so you can be near Grandma before she goes into the hospital tomorrow. She is sick with cancer: no more breasts, half a lung. She plays solitaire, sitting on her barstool; you sit next to her, careful not to disturb her game. A soft yellow light blankets the kitchen. The woven green place mats and checkered napkins are already set out on the bar for tomorrow's breakfast, along with a container of sugar substitute and the wooden salt and pepper shakers.

Grandpa keeps hundred-dollar bills folded tight in his money clip, which he tosses on the bar when he comes home, next to his diamond wedding ring, Swiss Army knife, and loose change. He sits in the living room and swears at the television. His leather recliner is off-limits, sacred, "Grandpa's chair." He watches *Jeopardy!* at high volume and drinks a martini with an olive speared on a toothpick. When he goes to the bathroom, you walk over and turn the television down.

Your grandfather goes to the kitchen to make another martini. An ice cube falls and slides across the yellow kitchen tiles. He picks it up and chucks it into the sink. His eyes tear, and he rubs them with the back of his hand. He goes back to his chair and turns the volume up with his remote.

After your grandparents are asleep in their bedroom, you find her suitcase on the dryer, petite and ordered, her initials engraved near the leather handle: DGM. You unzip the suitcase, and as you open it, your fingers touch silk pajamas. You know she will wear her slippers with the fur puffs on top in the hospital. You leave a note in her suitcase: "I love you. XXX OOO XXX." (She always signs her letters to you with X's and O's.)

At 6 A.M. you hear the clink of silverware, the clearing of throats, and the rustle of a newspaper, but not one word between them. Finally the back door shuts. The house vibrates as the garage door opens, and Grandpa takes Grandma to the hospital.

## *2001*

Three Christmases after your grandmother's death, your grandfather walks slowly with his cane to the table for dinner. Your sons, Cole and Ry, age four and two, are already seated. You try to help Grandpa, but he shoos you away with his hand. When he sits, his chair falls over backward, and his head whacks the wall. You help him up, saying, "Stupid chair." The boys are laughing. You tell them to knock it off, and they fall silent when they see the anger in your eyes.

"I'm fine," Grandpa says, his hands on the table. His skin has a yellow tint. Your family stands for the prayer: "Good food, good meat, good God, let's eat." Usually the prayer makes Grandpa smile, but tonight his head hangs down.

You visit him often these days. Mostly you talk and he listens—until he dismisses you with a wave of his hand. He reads sexy Western novels. Sometimes you grocery shop for him. "Sweet rolls and vodka," he says when you ask what he needs.

## 2002

Another funeral for a relative you don't know or care about, but you attend because your grandpa wants you there. Your relatives are mostly strangers with familiar faces. You kneel next to your grandpa, and he holds your hand and says, "Well, what do you know," and wipes his eyes with the back of his other hand.

He places his flowers on your grandmother's grave instead of the newly deceased relative's coffin. He starts to tumble backward, but you catch him. People are watching. Usually he hates attention, but this time he seems to enjoy it. He taps his cane on Grandma's headstone. "I'll be with you soon, honey," he says. "I'm on my way."

You and your kids visit him at his second home in La Quinta. The sun is setting pink along the golf course. Grandpa cusses at the television—goddamn this, and goddamn that—but when the boys come running into the living room to say good night, he softens and says, "Get a load of that. I'll be."

He moves to the kitchen using his walker. His hand yanks at the light switch. He has trouble unscrewing the cap from a new bottle of Smirnoff vodka; he takes his pocketknife out and struggles with the plastic seal.

Later the sound from the television wakes you. Your grandfather sits in his chair wearing only his boxers, one hand holding the remote, the other a martini. He mutes the TV and tells you he's been watching the boys sleep, which strikes you as odd. When you check on the boys, they seem fine, sprawled on twin beds, breathing deeply. You go back to bed. Soon after, you hear Grandpa shouting. "Go to bed, God damn it! Go to bed! God damn you! Little fucker!" Your throat tightens. You hurry to the boys' room. Grandpa is making his way back to his bedroom, hands on the wall for support, and your shoulder grazes his arm as you pass.

Ry is lying on his stomach, his face in a pillow, trying his best to keep quiet; his body makes hiccup motions. You see blood on the bedspread first, a thick mess, and you find yourself hoping it's an old stain, but then you see the blood on the carpet. Ry is relieved to see you; he repeats, "My mamaaa. My mamaaa," arms out, blood down the front of his pajamas. The room smells like urine. You're hot and sweaty, and suddenly you know you will throw up.

"Mommy, I peed my underwear," Cole says. He sounds afraid.

"I'll be right back," you say, heading to the bathroom. "Give me one second."

On your knees, hands gripping the toilet rim, you vomit. We'll leave, you think. We'll leave and never come back. I hate him. I hate him.

When you come out of the bathroom, the boys are watching you cautiously. The cut is near Ry's chin, like a small open mouth. Cole is naked except for a dinosaur undershirt. His urine-soaked underwear lies in a mound on the carpet. A tacky portrait of your brother stares down from the wall. On the other side of the room is your portrait, unsmiling, head tilted. You're feeling sick again, memories colliding.

"I'm going to ask you a question," you say, kneeling next to Ry's bed, "and it's very important that you answer the honest truth." Your hands are shaking, so you set them on your thighs. "Did Grandpa hurt you?"

His eyes are full of horror and wonder. "I fell off the bed, Momma," he says.

"Grandpa yelled. He kept yelling."

You look to Cole for confirmation, but he remains silent, watching.

"Grandpa hurt my feelings!" Ry says and begins crying loudly.

That's better, you think. OK. I can do this. You pull Ry's bloody pajama top off and carry him to your grandfather's room. Cole follows, holding the tail of your shirt.

Grandpa turns on his bedside lamp. You stand in his doorway, Ry's legs wrapped around your waist, his fingers

gripping your neck. You can feel him staring angrily at
Grandpa. "He's hurt," you say. "I have to take him to the
emergency room. The cut is deep. He must have fallen off
the bed and hit his chin on the nightstand."

"Are you sure?" Grandpa says. He looks alarmed and
blinks. You know Ry is giving him a stare-down, safe in
your arms. "Jesus," Grandpa says to Ry, "I'm so sorry.
Jesus Christ, I'm sorry."

Give him time, you want to say. Your youngest holds
grudges. He does not forgive easily. But then Ry surprises
you. "OK," he says, his grip on your neck loosening. "OK,
Grandpa."

Grandpa tries to kill himself soon after that. Your mother
catches him in the garage in his maroon Mercedes SUV with
the garage door closed and the engine running.

"He's tried it before," Mom tells you on the phone, "but
he hears me coming up the driveway and turns the ignition
off. I told him it's not going to work with all the cracks and
vents in the garage."

### 2003

You visit your grandfather in the psychiatric ward. When
you were twenty, before you went into the recovery home,
you spent four weeks in a psychiatric hospital for alcoholism and depression. Now you're thirty-four and have been
sober for thirteen years. Grandpa is eighty-seven. He's code
5150, meaning he might be a danger to himself or others.
You were never 5150. He wears beige slacks and a dark
green cashmere sweater.

"You look handsome," you say.

"The people here are crazy," he says. "They scream all
night. I have no shower, no phone."

"You tried to kill yourself," you say.

He scans the room; then his eyes peer into yours. "Did
you ever try to kill yourself?"

A nurse carts a tray down the hallway. Someone screams.
You hear the noise of a television from the next room.

"They were afraid I was going to take my life," you say, and you pause. He knows "they" means doctors, psychologists, and counselors.

"Is that right?" he asks. There's surprise in his voice, but also something else, as if he's proud. "Did they make you go to all this goddamn group therapy?" he asks.

You tell him you had to go to countless group-therapy sessions; you never got used to it.

"Did they ask you whether the glass was half full or half empty?"

"Yes."

"I don't know whether it's half full or half empty. It's just a goddamn glass."

"I know."

The pay phone in the hall rings. A man answers, then drops the receiver. It hangs like a broken branch.

"I promised Grandma I'd look after you," you say, although he already knows this. "Grandma said it would be hell." The abandoned phone emits a caustic beeping. A nurse hangs up the receiver with a bang. "Grandma would want you to go out with more dignity."

"I know," Grandpa says sheepishly. "It's all gone. The house—everything." The family tried to convince him not to sell the home he built in Corona del Mar, but he did. After the sale was done, you attempted to comfort him about his choice.

"It's still in my heart," you say now, pressing your hand to your chest. "I have it inside." Even as you comfort him, you know that you are being manipulated.

"OK, then," he says, and looks at his lap. You can tell he wants you to leave.

His social worker, Sally, walks you to your car. "The alcoholics always break my heart," she says. "He's going to find a way out of here. And most likely he'll try to kill himself again."

Your grandfather gets out of the hospital using his connections and his money. He pitches back cocktails at the clubhouse bar by the golf course in La Quinta. If he had a choice, if there was a switch labeled LIVE and DIE, he would flick it to DIE.

The clouds cast patches of shadow on the mountains. There is a waiter who serves only your table. He stands to the side and watches while you eat. The busboy, a small Japanese man Grandpa calls Pee Wee, has been clearing your plates and filling your water glass ever since you were a tot. When he pours you more water, his hand shakes, and a little liquid sloshes over the side of your glass. Your boys are running around out on the putting green. "Stop kicking the flowers!" you yell.

Afterward, crammed into the golf cart with you and your kids, Grandpa lights a cigarette. Ry sits on your lap and watches Grandpa smoke. "You are making fire," Ry says. "Are you going to eat that stick?"

Grandpa gives him a deliciously crazy grin. You've seen this grin your whole life; it borders on cruel, but it still makes you feel wild with delight, and grief. With each of his self-killing acts, the drinking and smoking, you feel some measure of pride. Destructive behavior in the face of love is powerful, you think. To be loved anyway.

When you look into Grandpa's rheumy, miserable eyes, you sense that old death wish. This is our connection, you think. He knows I know. You do your best to not let the wish take hold and drag you down, but you feel it thump at your temples.

### 2004

Marsha the nurse says Grandpa can hear you, even though he's in a coma. "This is the best he's been all day," she says. She turns Grandpa on his side. Marsha is a gregarious, hefty woman with a large diamond wedding ring. Since you've been here, you've seen her consume a smelly burrito and a pound cake. She sucks saliva out of Grandpa's mouth with a tube and talks about the Lord taking each person when the Lord sees fit. You are alternately revolted and comforted by her.

Grandpa is wearing a neck brace. He was drunk and stoned on antidepressants and pain medications when he fell and broke his neck. An oxygen mask covers his nose and mouth, and there's a milky glaze over his eyes. You hold his hand and talk to him. If he weren't in a coma, he would probably tell you to be quiet and leave. Grandpa does not like too much togetherness. Voices come from the nurses' station: two nurses talking about last night's episode of Sex and the City.

"Do you want to be my Luvah?"

"That's exactly the way he said it!"

Marsha pokes her head between the curtains. She says his body is shutting down, points out how his toes and fingers have turned purple. "He must have been amazing in his day," she says.

On January 7, at 6:18 P.M., your grandfather dies while you are holding his hand. His eyes shift quickly to the right, and pivot back. Marsha comes in and confirms his death. "It's over," she says, fingers on his wrist, feeling for a pulse. When she looks away, Grandpa's eyes shift and pivot back again. He is beginning to turn yellow.

Marsha flips through his chart and makes notes. "Boy, he kept on trucking after you arrived," she says. "He must've really loved you."

You nod.

"He was very resilient," she says, and her big thighs make a rustling noise as she walks past. "Lucky you," she says distractedly, pulling a sheet over Grandpa. "You get his genes."

# SUNSET BOULEVARD

## Stephen Jay Schwartz

When I was ten years old my father, a respected pediatrician, pulled me aside and nervously announced that he had some things to discuss with me. I stared up at him, waiting. Finally, he handed me a black-and-white pamphlet titled *Doctors Talk to Nine to Twelve Year Olds*. "Read this," he said, and quickly left my side.

Two weeks later he stopped by my room and asked, "Did you read that thing I gave you?" I had to search my memory, and then I glanced at the pamphlet buried under my desk. I remembered opening the pages, seeing line drawings of a penis and vagina. The images embarrassed me and I quickly tossed the book aside.

"Oh, yeah, I read it," I lied.

"Good," he said, and walked away.

That was the extent of my sex education. Sex was never again discussed in our household. It was treated as a great, shameful mystery. And yet, as a young pubescent, I was aware that something strange and different was happening around me. I saw images of near-naked women on billboards and in television and print ads. I remember once I was taking out the garbage and I found a bloody bundle of toilet paper. I was concerned that someone might have been hurt and I rushed to my mother to ask her what happened. I received a curt, angry response and was told to mind my own business. Somehow I felt ashamed for having asked the question, and I was vaguely aware that it had something to do with this thing we never discussed, this thing called *sex*.

As a child, I experienced no terrible, traumatic event. I simply lived a cloistered life regarding sexuality, and I had the vague idea that sex was naughty, dirty and wrong. As I entered puberty I became naturally more intrigued about it, but, at the same time, I came to feel there was something naughty, dirty and wrong about *me* for thinking about it.

When I was fourteen, my father left my mother to marry a woman ten years his junior. The crisis this caused in my life was quiet and hidden. I was a healthy, outgoing teenager with plenty of friends. But my father's departure left a hole in my life, and an insecurity, and a deep desire to be needed and loved. My brain translated this emotional need into a physical one. I became sexually active immediately, awkwardly experimenting with the girls I knew, touching, exploring. I lost my virginity at age fifteen with a girl the same age. I remember apologizing to her afterward.

"I'm so sorry, I'm so sorry... I didn't mean to do that, I hope it was okay with you..."

She looked at me and smiled. "Don't worry, it's what I wanted, too."

We lay together on the couch, her parents asleep upstairs. I was excited that we lost our virginities together, as boyfriend and girlfriend. It seemed so perfect.

"Was that your first time?" she asked, coyly.

I felt my stomach sink. "Of course," I said. "It was your first time, right?"

She leaned into my shoulder comfortably. "Nope. I lost my virginity when I was fourteen, with Devon."

Devon was a mutual friend at school. I didn't even know they knew each other. Suddenly sex seemed very important. I realized I had to up the ante. Over the next six months my girlfriend and I had sex two to three times a day. This didn't seem too different from what a lot of teenagers were doing at the time. But I seemed to need it more—not necessarily the sex, but the attention, the comfort, the connection. After that relationship ended I went from one girl to the next, usually falling head-over-heels in love. When a relationship ended I felt crushed. Abandoned. I needed to dive into another one immediately.

When I was twenty my father committed suicide. For me, this produced two immediate responses: one, my writing suddenly matured—I now had issues to explore in my life that were too important to suffer immature writing—and two, my search for a romantic connection led me to cross a line between normal sexual behavior and a type of behavior that ultimately became compulsive, dangerous and illegal.

I'd always been intrigued by prostitutes. I'm a fan of Charles Bukowski and Jack Kerouac and Henry Miller. I'm fascinated with lives lived desperately on the edge of society. I romanticized life on the street and felt that a "real" writer would know the world of prostitutes first-hand. I remember a particular time, not long after my father's death, when, while driving along Sunset Boulevard, I noticed an attractive blonde on a street corner, her eyes tracking mine. It was the same kind of look I might have received from a girl sitting across the room from me in one of my college classes. I pulled over and rolled down the passenger side window, just to say hello, to smile and receive a smile in return. Suddenly, her hand was on the latch of the locked passenger-side door. "Hurry up," she said, "the streets are hot."

I unlocked the door and she sat down beside me. "Drive already," she said. I put the car in gear and took off, not knowing exactly what I had gotten myself into.

"What do you want?" she asked, impatiently.

"I... don't know," I said, "I just saw you on the corner and thought maybe you needed a ride..."

She looked me over, then smiled. "You ever done this before?" she asked.

I was silent, nervous. It made me think of that first girlfriend, when I lost my virginity. I was suddenly embarrassed. She put her hand on my thigh.

"What would you like?" she asked. Her hand moved up my leg.

"I...uh, maybe a hand job," I managed, avoiding her look.

She let her hand fall between my legs. "How much you got?" she asked.

I told her I had twenty dollars. She seemed to think about it before directing me to a street where we could park. We parked and I touched her full breasts over her sweater and she placed her hand in my pants. Seconds later it was over. I paid her, dropped her off on a different street corner, and drove on. I looked in my rearview mirror and realized that no one was following me. Police units did not come screeching around the corner. I'd just met a good-looking girl, got "lucky" on the first date, and the only consequence was that I was twenty dollars lighter. It seemed like a good deal to me.

I was now experienced, like the writers I admired.

My attitude was that this was a rite of passage, something every gutsy young artist should try. I didn't realize how deep this penetrated into my psychology. That it came from a hole in my life and this twenty-dollar experience had, for one brief moment, filled the hole.

A few weeks later, I found myself on Sunset Boulevard again. Something had put me there—some pressure I was feeling in school, or at work, or in the relationship I had with my girlfriend at the time. Instead of dealing with these issues head on I decided to run. I didn't seem to have the strength to fight. Maybe I felt there was no easy way out. Maybe I was running from my dad. Whatever it was, I realized those hours driving in my car was time dropped from my life, when I didn't have to think, or feel. They were cushioned, comfortable moments of nothingness. And yet, there was a purpose. Find that girl.

I remembered the blond girl and the brief experience and the excitement, the sense of danger and adventure. Nothing else seemed to matter. I knew my problems were out there, in the distant fuzziness of my mind, but then, in that moment, my problems didn't exist. Hollywood Boulevard,

Sunset Boulevard, Santa Monica Boulevard, Fountain, Franklin, La Brea, Highland. They were suddenly everywhere. Girls, on street corners. Lines of cars with single men at the wheel. Cops arresting girls, cops arresting johns. I'd see an attractive girl on the street and chicken out. I'd circle back and she'd be gone. I realized that if I didn't stop the moment I saw a girl, the guy behind me would. It was a seller's market. I was pissed at myself for having let the good ones slip by. Finally, after three or four hours, I'd see the "perfect" girl, pull over, and pick her up. The experiences were similar—secluded side streets, twenty or thirty bucks, hand jobs in the car—but none seemed as satisfying as the first. Each time I went out I made a mental note—this time I'll do a better job. I'll make it like the first.

And so it went. What had started as an "innocent" experiment turned into a compulsion and a secret life. I was on the street sometimes three, four times a week, cruising the boulevards for hours in search of the perfect connection. It was an elusive, misguided search, because the perfect connection didn't exist. Not there, at least, not on Sunset Boulevard.

This went on for years, even as I experienced supposedly healthy relationships with girls in and out of college. Sometimes I would stop cruising for months before something set me off and I'd find myself on the streets again. At some point I stopped looking in the mirror. I couldn't stand seeing the face of a liar. I prayed that God would help me stop. I'd go a couple of weeks without cruising and then it would begin again.

In the meantime, life went on. The "good" me, the one everyone knew, graduated from college and found occasional success as a writer and filmmaker. I had been in a long-term relationship and I was engaged to be married. I had a job as a development executive for a reputable film director. Things were looking good. When the High Holidays came around, I prayed that God would help me stop the cruising. I promised myself it would stop before my wedding day. It would have to. I wasn't going to be a cheating husband. I wasn't going to be like my father.

I don't remember how many months I lasted after my wedding day. I don't know what set me off. But something happened and there I was. Sunset Boulevard.

I knew no way out. I was too ashamed to tell anyone what I was doing. I was afraid it would get back to my wife and she would discover she was married to a fraud. My friends and co-workers knew me as a kind and loving person—it would kill me if they knew the truth. I often wished I would die, to save myself the embarrassment of being discovered.

When my wife became pregnant, I made another promise. I would stop this behavior before our child was born. I rationalized that I could lie to my wife—I'd lied to every girlfriend I'd ever had—but I could not lie to my children. It hit too close to home. My father, before he left my mother, had been secretly seeing his mistress for six years. It had started when I was eight years old. I realized that he had not only lied to her, he had lied to me. I might have been a terrible husband, but I was not going to be a terrible father.

I don't know how many months I lasted after he was born. Maybe six. Maybe it was a year. All I know is that I was out on the street, again, picking up prostitutes. I had learned to mix things up a bit, juggling the street girls with trips to strip clubs and massage parlors. I was lost, divided, filled with shame. The only way I could live with myself was to live as two different beings; one dark, one light. One face I showed to my wife, family and friends, the other I showed to the night.

Then one day my wife came back from the doctor's office to tell me that her gynecologist thought she might have an STD. Or it could have been a yeast infection. My wife said she told her doctor it was definitely a yeast infection, because the only person she had a sexual relationship with was her husband, and her husband was not the kind to cheat. In fact, her husband wasn't even that interested in sex, which had been a problem in the relationship for some time.

"An STD? Wow, that's crazy," I said uncomfortably. I couldn't look her in the eye. "I guess I should get checked up, too, then."

There was a long, quiet moment.

"Why would you have to get checked up if I have a yeast infection?"

I scratched the back of my neck, felt the sweat on the palm of my hand. My vision was getting fuzzy. My voice was a thousand miles away. "I don't know, I just thought... it would be the right thing to do, to be supportive." I didn't even know what I was saying. I was talking just to talk. I never imagined that a bridge connected the person my wife knew and the person I hid on the boulevard. And now, suddenly, there it was. All I wanted was to drift away.

My wife didn't challenge me that night. She went to her doctor the next day and underwent a number of tests. Soon she discovered that she had, in fact, a yeast infection. I went through a number of tests as well and discovered that I did not have an STD.

If I'd only kept my mouth shut, I thought. What have I done?

My wife couldn't shake the feeling that she had stumbled into something. She talked to her family and friends and they all agreed that she needed to confront me. She came to me one night with some questions.

"I don't understand why you thought you might have an STD," she said, slowly, watching my eyes.

"I... I just haven't had a check-up in years, you know... so I thought it would be a good time to..." She asked more questions, and the answers I gave made no sense. This thing I'd been doing, all these years, seemed like fiction to me. It didn't exist in the real world. And yet...here I was. My wife was asking questions, and I was lying to save my life.

My lies were fat and thick and repulsive. They started small—"I went to this massage parlor once and had a hand job and I was afraid that I might have picked up an STD." Then another question would stump me, and another lie evolved, and it would contradict the first. My wife could not discern truth from lie. She wondered who she'd been married to all these years. I said, "I'm telling you the truth, trust me. What do I need to do to prove I'm not lying?" Her answer was right there, as if she'd been thinking about it for days. "I want you to take a polygraph test."

I was far away in my head. I barely heard what she said. But I knew I had to answer correctly. "Sure, sure, you're right, I agree. Great idea."

"Good," she said, although I could hear the doubt in her voice.

She found an investigator and scheduled the test for the next week. As the day of reckoning neared I wondered if I could beat the test. Maybe there was some special trick. A few days before the test my wife told me she didn't want to hear any more lies. I had one last chance to tell her everything, and the test would simply confirm what was said.

At this point I accepted that my marriage was over. I knew I'd lose my children, my wife, my home. If there was a bottom, I was about to hit it. I had nothing more to lose because everything was lost already. Nothing was holding me back now from letting go, from being honest. And I desperately wanted to be honest. Isn't this what I'd been praying for, after all?

I made the decision to tell my wife everything, every detail if she wanted to hear it. She wanted to hear it. And so I did.

I told her all the things I had done, over all the years. She became obsessed with knowing the specifics. I told her everything I could remember. She was shocked. I was shocked. I'd never told anyone about this, and now I was telling my wife every detail. If the story was about someone else I would have found it fascinating. Unfortunately, it was about me.

She kicked me out of the house. I was certain she had kicked me out of her life as well. I came back to take the polygraph test, which I passed, confirming that I had told her the truth about all the lies I had told her before. Now she knew what she was dealing with. Now she knew the whole truth.

We went through a period of weeks where I would come whenever she called and we would talk and I would answer her questions. As terrible as I felt about myself, I also felt free, for the first time in fifteen years. The weight from this terrible secret was lifting off my back.

To my astonishment, my wife suggested that we see a marriage counselor. We ended up talking to someone at Kaiser who listened to our story, who heard my wife cry and plead while I sat looking guilty and sad, agreeing with everything my wife said. During the session my wife referred to me as an adulterer. The therapist turned to her and said, "Don't think of him as an adulterer. Think of him as an alcoholic."

It was a watershed moment.

An alcoholic? What did that mean? She suggested I attend a meeting. She gave me a phone number for Sex Addicts Anonymous. Oh, my God, was I a *sex addict*? Some part of me preferred to be an adulterer. Sex addict sounded... creepy.

I attended my first meeting and was surprised to discover that no one appeared particularly creepy. They were businessmen, lawyers, doctors, religious leaders, mechanics, students, actors, policemen...in short, everyone. The thing they had in common was the thing I apparently had, an addiction to sex. And there were women in the room, too. This was bigger than I knew, a secret epidemic that had somehow eluded my observation. It wasn't just about celebrities or politicians "getting a little action on the side."

I threw myself into the therapy. I attended meetings once, sometimes twice a week, went to private therapy, marriage counseling, and a small group therapy session for sex addicts led by two professional sex therapists. I read all the books, I got a sponsor, I did the Steps. I got my year "chip," followed by another polygraph test to confirm my "sobriety". I passed again and my wife and I determined we were on the right track.

At this point I decided to pull away from the film business. I realized that failing to find success as a screenwriter contributed to my lack of self-respect. And that led to a spiraling sense of doubt and depression, which led to acting out. I decided to write short stories and practice my craft. As I continued my therapy I came upon the idea of writing a novel. I realized that if I had read a novel, say, a popular thriller whose protagonist just happened to be a sex addict, I might have discovered, years earlier, that what I was doing was "acting out". I might have recognized my behavior in the pages and learned that this nightmare was called "sex addiction", and there were places I could go for help. Like meetings.

So when it came time for me to write my first novel, I decided to write what I knew. The writing became a "check-in", a way to examine where I was in my recovery on a daily basis. I was struggling with the Steps, so my character struggled with the Steps. I had to take a polygraph test, so my character had to take a polygraph test. Writing the book gave me a voice, a way to stand up for myself in a way I never did before. Addicts have a difficult time telling others what they need, so when the pressure builds they find a way to self-medicate instead of facing their problems. I was able to explore these issues in my book, using a fictitious character as my alter-ego. Writing the book helped me through the process and, to a certain degree, kept me sober. But so did the honesty I shared with my wife and the incredible support she was giving me. And, if all that wasn't enough, there was the polygraph test to keep me true.

That novel I wrote became *Boulevard*, a dark crime-thriller about an LAPD homicide detective struggling with his sex addiction. He's an imperfect hero, some might call him an anti-hero. I call him human. He goes to meetings, has a sponsor, gets thirty, sixty, ninety days of sobriety, then falls off the wagon and starts over at Day One. In the story, he investigates a series of crime scenes and discovers that the killer knows who he is, and, in particular, knows he's a sex addict. The killer has been to his meetings. Suddenly my protagonist has a whole lot to lose.

Writing the book was a catharsis for me *and* my wife. She's an accomplished story editor and she fell in love with the story as I was telling it. She saw the flawed character and realized I had touched upon something real and universal. She pushed me to delve deep into my memories in order to present the world as it really was. It was a tough line for both of us to walk. She felt strange encouraging me to relive those moments in my mind, and I struggled with how these memories tempted me to act out. The dynamic produced a strange and beautiful new relationship, founded on trust, creativity, and mutual growth. I discovered that my wife was interested in seeing the full dimension of the man she'd been married to for fifteen years. The dark and light had come together and she now faced a real, three-dimensional human being. She was willing to give our relationship a shot if I was willing to stay honest and put in the necessary work.

It's been seven or eight years since I acted out in my Inner Circle. I've actually lost count. For many years I stopped going to meetings. I figured I was better, one of the success stories. Then something happened that caught me off-guard. I discovered Internet porn. So, for over a year I found myself with a new struggle, an Internet addiction. To me, Internet porn had never been a big deal—I thought of it as simply an endless *Playboy Magazine*. My problem had always been with real, live women. But that changed as I clicked from image to image to image. Ultimately, this resulted in a problem with intimacy in my marriage. I disclosed what I was doing and we started the process again—a return to the meetings, another polygraph test, a few more checks and balances in order to get things back on track.

Addictions are sly little devils. They wait in the wings for an opportunity to attack. I needed a combination of things to finally help me break the cycle. Individual therapy, marriage counseling, a loving, supportive partner, and twelve-step meetings. The meetings were key. They saved my marriage, and possibly my life.

Addictions are a life-long struggle. I suppose I could have been any kind of addict. As a compulsive person I could have found cigarettes, food, drugs, self-mutilation, alcohol... who knows? I just happened to be wired for sex.

For many years I felt terrible about my life. For many years I felt I'd rather die than let my secret out. I often think about my father, who struggled with depression and eventually killed himself. I've always thought that if he'd just gone to therapy, if he'd waited those tough times out, he would have made it through to the other side. He would have been around to share life with his kids. He would've met his grandchildren. And if I had ended my life fifteen years ago, I would never know the life I have today. A rich life. A layered life. An honest life. One I can share with my wife and kids. The cycle of shame has been broken.

# 23

## John Amen

That birthday, I swallowed Valiums with vodka,
drove dark back-roads, both headlights broken.
I made it to the driveway, crashing into an oak,
passing out behind the airbag. Jul called an ambulance,
and I came to in intensive care, sunlight flooding
through barred windows, tubes flowing like power lines.
I'd been here before, each survival bolstering some
myth of invincibility, but this time I knew I was treading
a bloody shark pool, the inglorious end converging like teeth.
I told the doctor I intended to get clean. He shrugged
when I declined his offer to check me into a treatment center,
railed that the odds were mounded against me. Death
sat on the edge of the gurney, smiling like a mentor.

# THE WORLD BREAKS EVERYONE

## Ruth Fowler

I gravitated to the fucked-up writers. Hunter S. Thompson, Hemingway, William S. Burroughs, Raymond Chandler, Tennessee Williams, Dylan Thomas, Jack Kerouac, Truman Capote, Charles Bukowski, William Faulkner. There weren't many women in my list. Dorothy Parker, and that was about it. Somehow, hand in hand with booze and drugs, the terrible dance that substances led me on became one that I must perfect to be a writer. It was a required necessity, an essential rite of passage, and my writing heroes' words were the proof. I drank, gurned, snorted, swallowed and hallucinated like they did. That waltz into the dark was absolutely crucial for me in order to write like them—even if the familiar, haunting beautiful chimes of The Blue Danube led me instead to the depths of degradation, I could still write about it.

*Once I was arrested on a highway in Portland Oregon, suspected of fellating the driver of a moving vehicle. Once I screwed a man twenty years older than me on the top deck of a yacht, not realizing that the crew were sitting downstairs, watching intently on the security cameras. Once I slept with a man and his brother in the same night, while their friend watched. Once my mother stabbed me with a fork. Once I danced naked like a pixie for a man thirty years older than me so that he would buy me drugs. Once I coerced a reference out of my Cambridge University tutor, ostensibly for a university application, in reality so I could steam open the envelope and find out what she thought of my writing: 'Ruth is heartless—but perhaps that is a very good thing for a writer.'*

I lost my heart somewhere along the way, drowned with booze and addled by coke and shrooms. I wish I could get it back. *Ruth is heartless.* Terrible things, memories. Made flippant by necessity. To regard them with their full weight would make my non-existent heart burst. I only admitted to them with braggart and bravado in writing, in alcoholic top-trumps, when laughing removed the poison, their ability to wound. The taste of humiliation became a familiar one in my using years, but I integrated it into my words and turned it into a triumph, like Hunter did, like Bukowski did. Swirled in the mouths of others it was still painfully raw, distinct, sharp and new. "D'you remember...?" some asshole would say, not registering me cringing away from the howl of silent shame, "D'you remember when you scored coke off that rickshaw driver and fingered Stephanie in the hot tub before giving everyone lap dances?" I never let anyone else have that pleasure. I wrote about my own humiliations first, asking myself: What would Hunter S. have done? Oh, far worse. *We were on the edge of Charing Cross Road when the cocaine began to take hold. I think I said, "Paul, get the fucking rickshaw driver to take us to a crack den..."*

I traveled all over when I left university with a remarkably good degree, considering I had been snorting coke off the back of 'Sir Gawain and the Green Knight' every morning to help me stay awake when revising. I drank in London, I starved myself in Argentina, I swallowed MDMA in Alpe D'Huez, snorted coke in Antibes, drank copiously in Nice, screwed strangers when high in Monaco—but I merely drank in the Caribbean, locking myself away on the boat I was working on, convinced that if only I did not escape during the full moon, I could not hurt anyone else. I was only a werewolf if others witnessed it.

It didn't work so well when drinking and drugs became a requirement to work, which is what occurred when I moved to New York, and visa held up in immigration, money running out, I procured gainful employment in a strip club. Gloria Steinem was a bunny girl, I told myself hopefully. And Hunter, I'm sure, would have *loved* Flashdancers and Scores. I had to drink to dance. Oh I'm sure there were many who could leap upon that stage wearing dental-floss panties buoyed by nothing stronger than a Sprite, but I was not one of them. Dancing required drinking, coke and embracing the darkness. I would write angrily at 5 a.m. after work on a blackout, my words roaring ferociously off the page, accusing the world for what eventually I had to admit was mine—culpability.

While gripped with self-loathing, there was still something darker inside of me that felt like this was proof I was an *artiste*. I wrote a book about my demise when I was twenty-six: structured beauty out of pain and degradation, but when my agent and editor asked for something more, I didn't know what to write. I knew only variations of the same story: *Girl in pain drinks and takes something—anything—to stop the feeling. Girl wakes up in more pain, is more angry. Girl does more to block it all out.*

It puzzled me that within this grand narrative I couldn't find the other tales that should be there: the ones about love and friendship, betrayals, victories, failures, loyalty. *I couldn't find them.* I'd type and type, a bottle of wine by my side, a wrap of something, a stolen pill, wherever I happened to be (Tobago, France, Italy, St. Maarten, Antigua, London, St Lucia, New York, Guatemela). And after my book came out—one long vicious wail—I was out of words, but I wasn't done with drink and darkness. I simply couldn't convey what was still happening to me, and I couldn't write about anyone or anything else. A sorry state of affairs for one who makes a living by writing prose about herself and screenplays about other people. I tried not to think about it. Drank more. Got my own dealer. We broke up. Kept moving. I had stayed too long at the fair, but it had not occurred to me that leaving might not be the solution. New York - London. London - Chicago. Chicago - Minneapolis. Minneapolis - Missoula. Missoula - Portland. And then Los Angeles.

By now I'd been fired from even my freelance gigs, and an argument with a publisher in England had ended by me walking out of a book deal with HarperCollins. My best friend sent me this email somewhere along the line, exactly when, I can't remember:

> *you're not a good friend—you're a bully. i dont want to hear from you again and i'd be grateful if you could respect that. i have deleted your previous emails and will not be either printing them out or even reading them. despite everything i wish you all the best with your new flat, the book etc. i am sorry you are so unhappy.*

*I am unhappy, I'm desperately unhappy.* Unhappy punctuated with pockets of OK. I wonder if she knew, or if she was just hopeful. People send emails like this because they want to wound deliberately, lash out to stop the pain, growl and bite like a dog protecting itself from a kick. Where you have wounded unintentionally, they wound intentionally merely out of self-protection.

> *I'm sorry I'm so unhappy too. I'm sorry I'm so angry. I'm sorry I'm such a cunt. I'm sorry I drink too much and take too much coke and swallow too many pills to make it all go away. I wonder what will stop it. I wonder if it's in me, or if it's all the things that have happened to me, the instability and the loneliness I stumbled upon. I'm sorry I'm so unhappy too, former best friend. I don't wish you all the best.*

I wish you all the best. This phrase turns up many times, this phrase, often in emails or messages from people who obviously *don't* wish you the best. They wish you herpes, syphilis, bankruptcy, and purgatory. I have teetered on the brink of suicide many times in my life, but what I think will truly send me down the route of that oft-planned heroin-overdose is when I become the kind of vacuous moron who parrots that phrase to people I despise: I wish you all the best. *No you don't, you lying, passive aggressive cunt.*

There are so many thoughts I needed to stop saying aloud. I needed to carve out the socially acceptable me who knows when to stay quiet, suppress leaking ink-blot thoughts, turn impulse into unarticulated flickers of thought, ignored, unexpressed. It would not happen when the only way I could control how I felt is by anaesthetizing it into oblivion.

Somehow, I ended up in Los Angeles, possibly on a blackout.

I remember sitting in someone else's million dollar home, somewhere in the stratosphere, money leaking like water out of my bank account, a gram of coke lined up before me, two MDMA pills imbibed, a cap or two of shrooms, an Oxy, several bottles of Veuve in the fridge. A rich fat man talks. I don't know him, but we are doing drugs together.

"So Richard Harris met Hunter S. Thompson and Johnny Depp to discuss a potential project together, but Hunter was absolutely fucked when he arrived. He was a nightmare. Loud and arrogant and railing against the world. Apparently he threw a dog out of the window, and eventually even Richard and Johnny had had enough of him, and asked him to leave. Hunter refused and so his chauffeur came in, and sprinkled a long line of cocaine leading from the house, to his waiting car. Hunter snorted the line all the way out the door—and then his chauffeur booted him in the back seat and drove off, to everyone's relief."

We don't know if it's true, but we laugh anyway. We are Hunter being led out of the door by a trail of cocaine which is never enough, everyone else sick of the sight of us, our glamorous reputations made ugly by proximity, and though we are neither successful nor revered, we don't let this deter us from the faux enchantment tingeing our tawdry evening. I found compadres in LA. We drank and smoked excessively, but it never felt frenzied or desperate or wrong. We all knew our youth was languidly flailing in the consistent and brutal assault of nicotine and booze, but in LA we didn't care, not enough to stop anyhow. We'd roll out of a different bed each morning like sorry reptiles—skin ashy, mouths glutinous and foul, skin damp and scaly—crews crawl to the fridge, start right back up again with an infliction of Corona, followed up with a defiling glass of chilled Pinot, maybe, if we felt kind, a sympathetic coffee.

Before I got in the car and drove down Sunset to Santa Monica, or Burbank, or Century City, or Malibu, or WeHo, or Venice, I'd chew gum like some insane fucked-up gurning meth-head, worried that the alcohol fumes roaring out of my mouth might deter the Producers I was meeting from buying my scripts. The meetings by day became merged and mangled into one another, so that I had a perfectly scripted set-piece that could be replayed on an interminable loop. It became a familiar sitcom, me the b-list bad actor, hungover with an inane grin and stupid stories vomiting out of my mouth. One time I rocked up early to meet with a film company on Wilshire Boulevard, wandered round the arid sidewalks past the Mercedes showroom, bumped into a group of paparazzi waiting hungrily outside a discreet celebrity hair stylist's for Ashley Tisdale. I quizzed them and we hung out together for a while, and it made me laugh, it was so perfectly fucking Hollywood. And that was the thing. It was all perfectly fucking L.A.; it was a perfect fucking time, full of perfect people laughing too loud and too long at my perfectly bad humor and telling me I was perfect fucking hot property. How can you argue with that shit? You can't, you just ride it, always knowing, sadly, with a hint of pre-nostalgia, that 'that shit' doesn't last forever, that with the crest of the wave comes the break, and all you can ever do is ride the surf, not ever be too sad at the inevitability of the end.

I drank some more. The rich fat man paid for my drugs and champagne. Fell out with my compadres. Stopped writing. Stopped caring. There was a sense somehow that I was removed or detached from the consequences of my actions. I suffered alcohol cramps and stomach pains, was unable to digest food so stopped eating, but with sustained effort rode through it and mastered my body by beating it into drowned, sodden, exhausted submission. I kept drinking more and the days and nights and drinks became indistinguishable, punctuated by a sleep that was sordid and alcoholic, uneasy and restless, and I'd wake up and start where I left off, and drown all the shit that was buzzing around in the background, a crackle of static, push it away and indulge instead in this smudged, crapulent, beautiful mess.

I can only describe L.A. in terms of disconnected snapshots, scents, images: sea air and sand and flip flops and shorts and cigarette butts discarded carelessly next to too-many empty bottles of booze, empty ziplocs, long, long nights talking, bruised kisses and pleasure and pain. I was treading a thin line between being inebriated and being a rolling, incoherent, dribbling, babbling, vomiting mess, and I can only attribute my failure to succumb to this increasingly alluring state, to my—by now—phenomenal alcohol tolerance and the ever-present wrap of coke on my person.

By the end, after the fury, when I knew that I had to make a choice, there was a gentle sadness in my drinking, a communion of sorts, a sense that if I only stayed here, reissuing the same conversations over and over, replaying the same goddamn movie reel, the sun would never rise and the night would last as long as I wanted it to, simply *because* I wanted it to. I could not write anymore, and I could not read. Words were now inadequate and approximate elegies for emotions so specific I could tell I had not felt them before, and had spent most of my life trying to.

I think, in all honesty, I was dying, and my words failed me.

I had to choose between writing and drinking. I chose writing. I did not write a word for eighteen long sober months. My words failed me again. I started to worry that by quieting the demon, I had exorcised whatever was in me that made me write. And then miraculously, when it was nearly over, in one six month mad sober flurry, I wrote two plays, two screenplays, signed with a new agent, and completed half of my second book.

Sometimes feeling everything so acutely is unbearably painful. Without the soft, alluring cushion of alcohol and drugs the colors are brighter and the edges are sharper. The words don't scream but instead, quieter, they have nuance and shades which I could not have recognized before. Sometimes it makes me unhappy, sobriety. Sometimes I still feel deep shame and horror at the things I did in those dark times, sadly intent on the mistaken belief that embracing blackness, jumping off that cliff, welcoming the fall, the impact of earth punching body, would make me wiser, or better, or smarter, a 'real' writer. Sometimes I believe it was invaluable to me, to who I am today, to everything that I now write. Sometimes I want to go back, but wonder if I can ride the wave right to the end, or whether it will break, and I'll be left floundering in soupy water, staring at the high-water mark in mute incomprehension, bitterly regretting I didn't just stay miserable someplace else, lamenting the sheer fact of trying. Most of the time I want to walk away from this sordid, nightmarish, alcoholic time forever and have it there in my memory just as it was, encapsulated and complete, perfect and untainted by a later edit.

# A BETTER PLACE TO LIVE

## Maud Casey

It's March 1999, two months since I stopped wishing I was dead. I read my mother's journal as I ride the F train to the end of the line in Queens—179th and Hillside—to the psychiatric hospital where I spent most of the last summer due to manic-depression. Surprisingly—as I come from a family of relentlessly nosy writers who believe anything not under lock-and-key is free game—I have my mother's permission to read her journal that spans my hospitalization and the five-month depression that consumed me after my discharge. I am doing research, trying to find out what the experience of my depression was like for other people. After my release from the hospital—once I no longer believed that the hospital staff was training a twenty-four-hour surveillance camera on me in order to eventually kill me—I was supposedly ready for the world. But was it ready for me? This is no saintly investigation, no purely altruistic walk in other people's shoes. The subject is still very much me, me, me.

Now that my depression has started to lift, I'm suffering from what I've come to think of as the hangover of the depressed: shame. I crawl out of bed some mornings like someone who has just woken up from a bender. I look in the mirror and think: Oh God, I did *that*? Who saw me? Maybe they won't remember; maybe they were really depressed, too?

This train ride is penance. My mother's journal is balanced on top of my own notebook, which teeters precariously on one knee. I—a former small-town girl who frequently falls *up* stairs and certainly no expert subway-riding-drinker-of-coffee—have a pen in one hand, a sloshing cup of coffee in the other, and the inevitable happens: I spill the coffee all over my mother's journal and the crotch of my pants. The man next to me rolls his eyes and moves away, wanting no part of this, but the woman across the aisle digs Kleenex out of her purse and hands them to me, shaking her head at the chaos in my lap but smiling sympathetically like someone who frequently finds herself cleaning up other people's messes. Above her head is an ad for Maple Gardens, a private rental community with a twenty-four-hour manned gatehouse. There are festive pictures of people in bright clothing playing golf, chatting poolside, and jogging cheerfully on treadmills. "You can't find a better place to live," the caption reads. I wipe coffee from my mother's words: *I feel Maud's misery and fear packed inside my senses. I wake in terror, always close to tears at dawn.*

I spent the fall of this year, and into winter, sleeping with my mother. In my Dial-A-Mattress bed in Brooklyn, I clung to her, often wrapping an arm, heavy and dead as my gone life, around her waist. I inhaled deeply her scent like smelling salts bringing me briefly back into the world. My mother worked full-time as a documentary filmmaker in New York, rushed to Prospect Heights to cook dinners I would otherwise skip, and traveled back and forth between New York and her home in Illinois. I tried to absorb that energy, her life force, like a plant absorbs the sun. But I wasn't that pure. There was desperation in my clinging—a kind of *Invasion of the Body Snatchers* life-draining suck and I had become pure such, the alien pod.

*September 8, 1998: Sleeping with Maud in her bed. The feeling both of laying my motherhood at her disposal and being a sponge to her deep fears and despair. The moon beams down on her through the window. I often think of her child body, child self, the joy she brought, how fascinated we were by everything she did; her stately, majestic, orderly procession through her skills and speech and school. These images return to me now as premonitions of pain to come. I look at her darling baby child self as wounded, as shrinking, shriveling in the shadows of her future suffering. Yet when I wake up at night, my child (a twenty-nine-year-old woman, but childlike in her pajamas, in her petiteness, in her funny little haircut and the simple sound of her breathing) is still there, my Maud bathed in the moonlight.*

During the weeks my mother spent in Illinois, my sister would sleep over on occasional nights. In her white nightgown with lace fringe around the neck, she was a radiant beauty—a successful writer and magazine editor who had recently fallen in love. She was my fairy-tale princess and my tentacles slithered out of their alien pod, wrapping themselves around her.

"I want to go back to the hospital," I would whisper to my mother trying to sleep next to me. "I want to die." "I want to go home," I would say to my sister as she rolled over to hold my shaking hands. The three  hospital, death, home—became interchangeable. "Tell me what's going on," my mother would whisper back, her warm body charged and ready like a nightlight, glowing with the possibility of emergency. "Maybe you could move to Virginia, live in Dad's extra apartment," my sister would offer. And for a minute that would seem like the answer—if only it were possible for me to move and simultaneously leave myself behind in Brooklyn. Unfortunately, to be depressed is not to have words to describe it, is not to have words at all, but to live in the gray world of the inarticulate, where nothing takes shape, nothing has edges or clarity. A literal home was not what I meant.

Home was what my grandmother seemed to be talking about in the last months of her life. Here on the train, eighteen different combinations of antipsychotics, mood-stabilizers, and antidepressants later, I remember this. As my grandmother lay dying in the house she shared with her husband in South Hamilton, Massachusetts, she talked a lot about "going home." Would you like something to eat? Some water? More covers? Do you need to go to the bathroom? Her children and husband asked her these questions and she replied with stern practicality, "No, thank you, I'm going home." (In my version of the story, my grandmother wags her long, thin finger satirically at the asker, the way she always did to indicate that underneath her scolding, stern personality was an appreciation for the naughtiness of the world.) For my grandmother, home was not in South Hamilton anymore. Home wasn't even in her body. She couldn't be bothered with the mundane details of the living—all of this eating, drinking, keeping warm, going to the bathroom, getting up, lying down, staying awake, going to sleep. Home was elsewhere, in death.

In the blackout drunk of depression, home was elsewhere for me, too. Not in my apartment in Brooklyn where I felt like a guest in someone else's falling-apart life—unanswered phone calls, unopened mail, rotting fruit on the top of the refrigerator, and something unidentifiable and reeking inside, piles of dirty dishes, tumbleweeds of dust, books I didn't remember reading, furniture I couldn't remember buying, pictures of friends and family that seemed to belong to a stranger. Not in my father's extra apartment. Not in my mother's house in Illinois. Not under my psychiatrist's desk where I wanted to curl up and hide, resting my head on his sensible shoes. Not on my therapist's couch, waiting and waiting for, as Freud put it so succinctly, neurotic suffering to become everyday misery. Not in my body. Not in eating, drinking, keeping warm. Not going to the bathroom or lying down. Not in staying awake or going to sleep. Above the Kleenex woman's head, the glaring reds, nuclear yellows, and shocking blues of the Maple Gardens ad run together in a perky smear. Being depressed felt like living in a corpse, so being dead seemed like "a better place to live."

The depression that follows mania is rarely dealt with as aggressively as the mania itself. Once the hard throb of emergency is over, the presenting crisis passed, many people are left to deal with the depression that leaves them nostalgic for the wild, bucking panic of mania—in my case, all those revolutions to tend to, bombs to dismantle (in a moment of unintended irony, I called 911 from the hospital), all those actors playing my friends and family. This hospital is really a whorehouse fronting for a drug cartel, isn't it? No, come on, you can tell me. It is, right?

During my depression, I often thought of something a secretary once said to me as she explained my duties as a temp, leading me through a fluorescent-lit office with no windows where I was to spend the next few months. It's not hard, she said, but it makes you want to shoot yourself. The lifetime risk of suicide among manic-depressives is 10 to 15 percent. Every morning before I went to work as an administrator in a theater school (a job I managed to keep despite all of my efforts to quit—my incredibly patient and kind boss wisely told me I should hang on until my medication had been worked out), my mother and her girlfriend counseled me, in person or over the phone. I can't go, I would say. I can't leave my apartment. I can't get dressed. I can't take a shower. Take a shower, they would say. Put on your clothes—remember your favorite black pants? The green sweater you bought when you first moved to New York? Find your wallet. Your keys. Walk out the door and lock it behind you. Buy a seven-day Metrocard, they would say (*because you can last that long*, they meant). Get on the 2 train, switch to the 4 at Nevins, and ride it all the way to Union Square.

Once I'd made it to work, I made lists: pills, suffocation, subway, bus, cut my wrists. I was forever staring at the tender blue veins along the inside of my wrists, fragile twigs trapped under ice. "Whatever happens, promise me you won't kill yourself," my best friend pleaded. "If you commit suicide, I'll kill you," my mother told me.

*September 21, 1998: Everything we worked for gone. She's slipped from being a high-functioning, promising, her-whole-life-ahead-of-her-young-woman to being someone beginning a downward grind. We'll have to take her home as a kind of second-class citizen.*

When my father's twenty-seven-year-old godson shot himself, it had seemed to me like the mysterious act of a grown-up who had seen things that I, at the age of eleven, hadn't. But even then I knew those mysterious things might be waiting for me, and when I as two years older than he would ever be, I could understand the general impulse: Let me out of here! Let me out of this body! I want to go home! But then there was my father visiting me for the day, reduced to tears by my own self-hatred. "I have nothing to say because I don't have any thoughts in my head anymore," I told him over and over. And my mother busting into one of my therapy sessions, a maternal terrorist, demanding that my therapist convince me to stay at my job, that she force me to understand that I didn't actually want to go back to the hospital. "She'll go back to that hospital over my dead body!" And my sister's voice over the phone, stripped of its usual joyousness, smooth and basic as the bone it had become: "Do you know how horrible the hospital was for you? For all of us?" I limited myself to banging my head against the wall, pinching and scratching my twiggy veins for relief.

Trapped in the dead body of depression, I was able to find relief in touch—the touch of friends and family who wanted to keep me from hurting myself as well as from the pain I inflicted on myself. As I clung to my job at the theater school, an institution steeped in the Method, I found myself using the same sense memory—an exercise that allows an actor to create reality through the memory of touch, taste, sight, sound and smell in the otherwise imaginary circumstances of an empty stage—that I described to potential students during interviews. A childhood friend—her mother lying in a hospital in Virginia after a near-fatal accident—came to *my* apartment and tickled *my* arm, stroked *my* hair as I stood mutely grateful. Her touch reminded me of the power of wordless physical connection, of what I would lose if I died.

One night, my best friend from college, disappointed that I had returned from the hospital (where she had visited almost every day) not closer to her but farther away, convinced me to have dinner with her at a loud, clattery restaurant rather than rush home to sleep. We sat opposite each other on long benches shared by other people, including a new, crooning couple next to us feeding each other noodles. My friend told me she wasn't sure what to do anymore, that she didn't know how to help me. Why wasn't I calling her? Why wasn't I sleeping on her couch, watching videos and letting her cook me dinner? I started to cry for the first time in months, relieved at the way her words shot through my medicine haze like a needle into my heart. As we held hands across the table, the anonymous buzz of people talking and laughing around us and our noodle-sharing neighbors oblivious, I remembered the specificity of friendship and was glad to be able to offer her my tears.

Sleeping next to the live bodies of my mother and my sister reminded me that I, too, had been alive once.

*October 3, 1998: I am completely braced to do whatever necessary to bring Maud through. I have the clearest feeling of being supported by recent years of happiness (lest anyone mistake me for a selfless person). Packed with satisfaction and strength, I've lived out a lot of things I wanted to do so that it's possible for me to be at her disposal. This feeling pours out for the most part (with occasional moments of self-pity), I will lay my fat years at the*

*service of her lean one. I have a sense of the depth of
the emergency. A visual image of the hollow beneath
her.*

I put my mother's journal and my own notebook into my
bag and stand in my coffee-soaked pants to look at the
subway map. The Kleenex woman looks up from her book
with a momentary flash of concern but then returns to her
reading. She's got her own destination. One hundred and
seventy-ninth and Hillside is three stops away. In my head, I
say the names of the people who rode this train to visit me:
Jane B., Janet, Nell, Julia G., Jeremy, Lorraine, Alex, Annie,
Jacob, Dwight, Cree, Sofia, Lenore, Rick, Daniel, Rose,
Matilda, Molly, Caitlin, Linda T., Steve, Connie, Harold,
Helen, Olivia, Virginia, Mike, Bliss, Jan. This list is like an
incantation, a poem I have memorized. I have filled entire
pages with these names, afraid afterward that I've left
someone out and afraid of the list itself, which still has the
capacity to split me wide open with humiliation. Like
someone who tells her most secret of secrets as she dances
naked and drunk in front of everyone she knows, I can
never be exactly sure what I revealed. Then there are those
who called, who wrote, who saw: John, Ros, Claire, Julia
C., Johnny, Lydia, Craig, Linda B., Van, Bruce, Tim,
Meredith, Jesse, Tracey, Darcey, Jane H., Tammy,
Benjamin, Lily, Eve, Nava, Meg, Carolyn H., Nancy, Pat,
Victoria, Anna, Carolyn T., Thomas, Elizabeth. I can't
remember them all. If I could only name all of them I might
gain some control over what otherwise feels like a stadium
full of people who witnessed this moment of skinlessness.
We are at the end of the line.

Hillside Avenue is a grim strip of discount electronic
stores and check-cashing places. Discarded fast-food
wrappers and sheaves of newspaper blow chaotically down
the street. While my mother was in New York taking care
of me, she became obsessed with the everyday trash that
found its way into the streets.

*November 11, 1998: The streets are flooded with litter but most people have washed and dressed themselves in clean clothes. They pick their way through garbage, as if they had nothing to do with it. People make their way along the junky street, transcending the plastic wrap, wax paper, underwear, intent on getting to the office, to their apartment. This morning, when Maud opens her eyes, she is restless and burning with self-hatred and fear. I can't, I'm stupid, I'm not able, no memory. She looks at me and says: You look nice. You're dressed as if there is nothing wrong.*

I stand in front of Liquor World and an off track betting parlor next to a group of teenagers—two boys and a girl. One of the boys is describing how the girl he went out with last night was so mad tight that it took him half an hour to get three fingers inside her. I flag a car and read from the tiny, coffee-splattered piece of paper on which I've scrawled the directions: *Hillside to Palo Alto, 1 block to hospital.* (I don't remember the trip here the first time—another childhood friend, whose brother had also been hospitalized, bravely and selflessly escorted me.) Hospital, home, death. I am finally going back to this place I'd claimed I wanted to return. As we pull into the circular drive of the hospital, a woman as thin as the sharp edge of a road sign stands outside smoking a cigarette. She seems familiar—it's as though we could be related. But the context comes back to me. She's one of the mental-health workers who held me down while I was being restrained.

"Hi," she says, stubbing her cigarette out on the hospital windowsill. "How are you?"

"I'm fine," I say. "Well, pretty good. Okay, I guess. You know, all right. So-so." What am I doing? I'm not wearing the right coat for this windy day and I've lost yet another pair of gloves. I want something from this woman. I want her to take me back. Wrested from the land of the living, I imagine myself sleeping the heavy sleep of sadness all day long—skipping groups, never changing out of my pajamas, and receiving only patients, like-minded people who understand best the desire to disappear from the face of the earth, as I lie in my sterile, white, clean hospital bed, running a salon for the insane. I want to go to a place where strangers take care of me, people whose pores are sealed, filled with their own rotten suffering. But I know better than that even before I walk back through the doors. Morning meds are at 8:00 A.M., if you aren't dressed, you are put on constant supervision, patients aren't allowed in other patient's rooms, and there are no such things as sterile, white, clean beds in a psychiatric hospital. At this hospital, you're lucky to get a pillowcase. Saying I wanted to go back to the hospital was akin to holding a gun to my head.

*December 3, 1998: I am hanging on by a thread. I want Maud to hang on to her apartment and her job, to stay in the world as proof that she isn't going to be ground down, smashed by her depression or marginalized, one of those cousins who Aunt Dora used to include at family holidays out of kindness. Don't forget—often these terrifying, destabilized events occur and you are completely on your own with no idea how to proceed even with people around you. What are analogous stories? Having a baby?*

Saying I wanted to go back to the hospital was like waving a gun around at everyone I loved.

Still, I try again. "I want to speak with someone about attending outpatient groups," I tell the security guard sitting at the front desk. He is a huge and grouchy man who doesn't look up from the screens in front of him, screens filled with the threatening stillness of empty corridors.

"Take a seat," he says.

My former psychiatrist—a jumpy, handsome man with a ponytail that serves as a barometer for his nerves—bursts out of his office on the first floor. His ponytail swings wildly behind him. He scans the room, sees me, and, being a man trained to head directly for trouble, heads my way. "What are you doing here?" he asks. He thinks I'm back.

For a minute I consider turning myself over to him, telling him I want to hurt myself so that he will be forced to act on my behalf. But shame burns through me like acid, and instead I say something about outpatient groups. He looks me up and down. "For you?" he asks incredulously. "For you to *participate* in?" He asks me about my current psychiatrist, my latest drug cocktail, whether I'm employed, where I'm living. I answer him—smart and kind, Tegretol, Wellbutrin, Effexor, yes, Brooklyn—leaving out the rest, the parts that hover between the facts such as how I can't figure out how to live in the world after preparing to give up for so long, how I'd gone to the edge and thrown all of my tools over, how the choices involved with living overwhelm me, how I just need to lie down on the old unit and rest for a little while until I feel ready to move back into my body. But he is shaking my hand, congratulating me, and then he sails off, his ponytail a wiggly rudder steering him onto the next crisis.

The grouchy security guard, his eyes still glued to the screens offering a filtered reality easier to bear, buzzes me through doors onto a locked unit so that I can use the bathroom. I go into a stall, sit on the toilet, and weep because I am not welcome here. They won't take me back. I cry mostly because this wasn't the place I'd been wishing for all along. Because what I really wished for was to disappear, and for the first time I see the tragedy of this as clearly as if I was the person lying terrified in my bed next to me or desperately trying to reach me across the table in a crowded restaurant. I cry briefly, efficient as the cold white tiles of the bathroom floor, and then walk back into the lobby where my psychiatrist hovers over a woman and her panicked daughter gesturing wildly. I call a car and go out into the cold gray day to wait. As I stand there, another psychiatrist, the man who performed my intake, strolls up the semicircle of the driveway. He recognizes me vaguely with the wary smile of a man who has seen thousands of patients come and go. I might have been his patient ten years ago or two weeks ago.

"How are you?" he asks, still moving toward the door. He knows just how much he can afford to give.

"Okay," I say, definitively.

He's partly through the door when, without breaking stride, he says, "It's cold out here." Exactly. He feels it, too. It's cold out here for everybody.

The car doesn't come for another half an hour. I wait alone in my too-thin coat and think about calling my sister when I get back to Brooklyn. Recently, she sent me an essay by Lauren Slater on depression. At first, I was unable— unwilling? —to learn about my own disease. It was mine, all mine! The idea of sharing, the idea of hope, seemed cruel. I had read Kay Redfield Jamison's *An Unquiet Mind* twice, and took a stab at William Styron's *Darkness Visible*, but they left me feeling even more depressed. How was I, a not-yet-published writer who didn't have the energy to turn on her computer supposed to feel better by reading the stories of depressed, famous writers? But, when I finally came back to myself, remembering how often reading had saved my life, I sat down with the Slater essay.

In the margins of the copy my sister had sent me—the copy she had intended to keep for herself—there were notes scribbled in her familiar, spidery handwriting. My therapist would probably remind me that there are no accidents, but, frankly, this can be an exhausting concept. I *wanted* to see. *Maud's second breakdown and later depression broke my heart in a way I'd never known, a loss that even now, with her back and healthy, I feel occasionally.* When I could breathe again, I began to see that the cruelty was not so much in the idea of sharing or the idea of hope as it was lodged in the layer of depression that is selfishness. My depression was not all mine, and as I read my sister's words again and again, relief loosened my relentless grip on my illness even as my heart broke, too.

When I call my sister, I won't tell her about this trip to the hospital. Not yet, I want to wait until the story is a gift and not a burden. Instead, I will tell her about a dream I had the other night in which we were the adults we are now wandering through my grandmother's Rhode Island house—a converted barn with beautiful high ceilings and an enormous window overlooking Narragansett Bay. The Barn, as it was called by our family, no longer exists. My grandmother sold it, and in a perfect symbolic gesture of resistance to its new owners, it burned to the ground. In the dream, my sister and I wander in my grandmother's garden and we come upon myself as a child, pudgy and tan all over from never wearing clothes. We squeeze my squishy child legs and then my child self tells us she's happy. But my sister doesn't hear and my child self runs away, turns into one of the groundhogs that plagued my grandmother by biting the heads off her petunias, and scurries toward the bay. I decide to leave out the part about my child self and just tell my sister about visiting the Barn, how beautiful it was in the sepia tones of dream memory, how blissful it was to wander in the long-ago garden with her.

I check my wallet for carfare and pick the trash—gum wrappers, pens that don't write, paper clips—out of my bag. These mundane details of the living make up the sweet straightjacket of practicality that holds me to the earth. In my mind, I wander through my Brooklyn apartment, where the dishes are done and the floors swept, looking for my gloves—the fifth pair I've lost this winter. I'll find them when I get home.

# ON THE OTHER SIDE

## David Huddle

of the shotgun you fired
into your mouth,

the wrists you slit
in a warm bath,

your swan dive
from the high rise,

the garden hose
you duct-taped

from exhaust pipe
to car window,

        and even
the pills you swallowed

and the plastic bag
you sealed around your neck,

                is the same hurtful,
                    pointless life

                you've always had,
                    it's like a blink,

a ten-second nap, and
dead, you wake up—

*voilá!* there it is,

your utterly

repulsive life,
your job, your clothes

that smell
like your unbearable body,

your hateful family,
your treacherous friends,

your despicable country, all
waiting for you

to get over it.

# NIGHT OF THE VIOLET UNIVERSE

## Rachel Yoder

He wore a blue button-down open at the neck and drove with one hand, careening down the narrow Georgetown streets. We sped by brownstones and iron gates, finely carved doors behind which lived diplomats and senators and the Secretary of State. He took me to a low-light restaurant where lilies and twigs balanced airlessly in elegant white vases. He spoke in Japanese to the bowing host and then surprised me after sushi with a flaming pineapple dessert.

"Happy birthday," he said, even though my real birthday was months away. The tiny waitresses sang in Japanese and then one snapped a Polaroid of me beaming with him beside me, his arm slung around my shoulders.

Three years earlier, I had come to the city from the dead end of a dirt road in the Appalachian foothills of eastern Ohio, from good Mennonite stock, raised to sew my own clothes, sing any part of four-part harmony, and navigate acres of woods by angle of light and sound of a creek. But the things I knew didn't matter in the city, where heavy-lidded Anglophones spoke in code: Patagonia. Tiffany. Martha's Vineyard. They wore strings of pearls and diagonally-striped ties. They drank wine. They ate brie.

He was one of them, or close, at least. Him, in shining Mercedes, wielding his credit card as we bushwhacked through the malls of northern Virginia. We danced barefoot in the grass at a Harry Connick, Jr. concert. He surprised me with a silver necklace cunningly stashed in the glove compartment. In Atlantic City we stayed in the honeymoon suite at the Hilton. In Florida, we had an ocean view from The Ritz.

On a sunny Saturday afternoon we lay on his bed and watched his favorite movie, an old 80s flick about a nerd who pays the head cheerleader to be his girlfriend. After, he played golden music and I lay on the bed, staring at him. Something was happening, a shimmer of glittering chemicals washed through me, every filament in my brain sparked and radiant. I felt as though a small, distant galaxy were turning inside. It glowed and murmured, swirled with stars. Little parts of me collapsed into its black holes. I laid there and asked him, did he mean to make me cry, and he asked, was I sad, and I said no, from happiness, had he meant to make me happy and crying like this? He shook his head and wrapped me up. He smelled of soap and hard candy, sheets and sleepy hair. He had these soft hands. His chest, it rode over him like sand dunes. He was pale and soft. He held me as tears rolled into my hair, *my baby, my baby*, wiping the wetness from my face, and kissing me, falling into me, the violet and gold haze of a universe swelling and shrinking, breathing as if alive. The curtains by the bed danced in the breeze.

I was twenty when I fell in love with this boy. Ten months later, I was sitting beside him on a 747 from Washington National to Phoenix, Arizona so I could check myself into treatment for love addiction. Love addiction. It sounds fake. But how do I explain what happened? What am I supposed to say? Vulnerable and young. Naïve. Impressionable. I was just this messed up girl. There are many ways to try and explain it, and none of them really make sense.

\* \* \*

If he thought my hair looked better curly and without highlights, then I let it air dry and took to growing out all the blonde. If he suggested I eat the primavera instead of alfredo, I changed my order. I liked my tube tops and short tight skirts, while he preferred button downs and fluttery, flowered knee-length dresses. I went to parties with endless cups of keg beer and called him late at night, slurring my words. He preferred I stay in, with him, not drink so much, or at all. I thought I was being friendly. He thought I was being a flirt.

After a back-to-school party on the university green, he started asking questions.

"Did you have fun?" he wanted to know. And who had I danced with? What parts of our bodies touched? What music was playing? That stupid rap music, was that what I'd danced to? Why did I like that music? And how much did I drink? How many cups? Who was there? What guys? Had I dated any of them? Which ones? When? Why? Did I love him? Why didn't I act like it?

We were in the bedroom by this point, talking across the bed. He kept asking questions. Was there a guy, some other guy? Some guy who I used to like?

"Did you talk to him?"

"I said bye."

"How?" he asked.

"Bye," I said, a buzzer going off somewhere deep in my head.

"That's it?" he asked. "You'd been drinking, Rach. No smile? No leaning in?"

"I gave him a hug," I offered.

"Rachel," he said. He made a point to sound reasonable, to keep his voice steady. "You just *hugged* him?" My face moved into hard positions. He opened his palms in the air.

"This is bullshit," I said.

"Answer the question," he said.

"I kissed him goodbye on the cheek," I said. He plunged his fingers through his hair and raised his face to the ceiling.

"I knew it," he said. "I knew it."

It had never occurred to me, none of this. My whole body burned.

"You make me sick," he said, turning from me.

I was of two minds. What had I done? How could I have been so stupid and slutty? But then, wasn't he being irrational and unreasonable, completely overreacting? I felt backed into a corner with only two equally unsatisfying options: agree I had betrayed him and beg for forgiveness, or try and argue my way out from under the disdain of the aspiring lawyer. It didn't occur to me to get up and leave.

"You kissed another guy!" he yelled, whipping his hands by his hips.

"It wasn't 'kissing another guy,'" I yelled back, trying to be firm but instead shrinking inside my clothes. "It was on the cheek."

"But flirty," he said, his voice no longer under control but taunting and mean. "Flirty, right Rach? You're so good at that."

"No, not flirty," I said weakly.

He paused.

"Show me," he said. I opened my mouth and breathed silence into the room. "Show me how you kissed him."

I stared at him.

"Show me or leave for good," he said.

Each of my bones liquefied, and my neck disappeared entirely. My head hovered in the air across from him, but he didn't notice. I wanted him to see how phenomenal I was, how magical, how I adored him, would do anything. Look, my head is floating.

"Show me," is what he said.

I stepped close to him, put my cheek to his, tilted my head, and touched my lips to his face. I pulled away and looked at him to see what had happened. I was crying.

"Do you see how you hurt me?" he asked. I ran to the toilet and threw up. After I flushed and rinsed my mouth, he was standing in the bedroom.

"Please don't dump me," I said. He opened his arms to me, and I collapsed into them, relieved. "Thank you," I whispered.

"You have to understand how much you hurt me when you do these things. You can't be like this. It's not right," he said as I sobbed. He was calm and quiet, stroking my hair. "I give you everything I have, I would do anything for you, and this is what you do—you hurt me."

"I'm so sorry," I cried. I was horrible. I was disgusting. I was not worthy of him.

\* \* \*

On his suggestion, I stopped drinking, began therapy, and threw out my rap CDs. I stuffed my tight clothes in white trash bags and watched them slide away down the garbage chute. I moved in with him, began taking pills, lost my appetite, tucked in bed for days at a time. I didn't leave the apartment by myself.

After months of his questioning and suspicions about my fidelity, I became terrified I would inadvertently cheat on him, and started having dreams about feeding chocolate-covered strawberries to handsome strangers. In the mornings, I'd awake to the boy staring at my face.

"What were you dreaming about?" he asked, sending me into a cold sweat.

During our marathon, late-night conversations, I'd sometimes black-out, my mind shutting off from too much anxiety and fear, simply blotting out what was happening and launching me into the only escape I had: sleep. I awoke in the morning in a pool of urine.

He just chuckled. "Oh, there's always something wrong with you."

And we continued to fight. I had smiled at the bagger boy at the grocery store. I had e-mailed a guy with whom I'd gone to high school. I hadn't joined in as whole-heartedly as the boy would have liked in his disparagement of an old boyfriend, or my father. "You're a slut," he yelled. "You're completely fucked up. You're a bad person. All you do is hurt me. I do so much for you, and this is how you act..." As punishment, he didn't talk to me. He left the apartment and wouldn't come back for hours. He pushed me, clad in my pajamas, into the hallway and locked the apartment door. When he let me back in, he put his hand on my head and kissed my cheek.

"See what it would feel like if I kicked you out?" he asked to confirm his point had been driven through.

By winter, our tunnel of love had grown dark. My old friends tried to help. They sat quietly in our old campus living room and each hugged me when I arrived.

"We're worried about you," they said. "Your whole personality has changed. We never see you." I set my lips in a mean line and stared at the ceiling.

"You don't understand. He's helping me," I said. "Plus, me changing has nothing to do with him."

They looked sideways at each other, and I stood up to leave.

There was no way I could explain anything to them. I was living in another country, far away from where they still were, from just months ago, the girl I used to be.

* * *

He and I endured our love as the winter snowed its way into early spring. Gray slush collapsed into mud along the sidewalks. The boy went to intern at the law firm while I slept in the apartment. The only thing keeping us afloat was the nights, the relief of nakedness and hands and skin. I wore black lingerie he'd bought for me, the lace loose around my disappearing body.

"Look how skinny you are," he'd say, running his hands over my thighs. "You look like a model."

"Like candy," I told him. "Like chocolate cake." I had a profound desire to consume him, to assimilate his physical body into mine. Barring this cannibalism, we made love, with the climax punctuated by me either breaking into waves of overwhelming laughter, or starting to cry, huge wet tears rivering down my face. We clutched each other like life preservers and, after, drifted together in bed until we fell asleep.

Even our physical chemistry could not prevent our inevitable descent though, to that dark night in February when, after being interrogated by him for hours over an old photo he'd found of me hugging a guy friend and of him kissing me on the cheek—Really? he said. Again?—I feared he was finally going to leave me for good. Estranged from my family, jobless, friendless, completely dependent on him for food and shelter, I literally had no place to go.

"You disgust me so much, I can't sleep in the same bed with you," he spat. I was sitting on the floor, blubbering, non-verbal. My head twitched, kicking back and forth. He pulled the cushions from the couch and laid them on the bedroom floor beside my half of the bed. "I don't know what you'll do to yourself if I leave you out here alone, so you can sleep on the floor in the bedroom. I want to keep an eye on you." Of course he did, I thought. I couldn't get away even if I wanted to.

I didn't sleep that night. I lay on the couch cushions and stared at the texture of the wall. I lifted the dust ruffle and looked at the darkness under the bed. I listened as he breathed in his sleep, somewhere above me. My muscles ached. My head was thick and clogged. I'd already vomited a few times. My skin itched. I was hot, running a fever.

Even worse, though, I couldn't stop thinking about what a level-headed decision it would be to kill myself. More calm than I'd been in months, I considered the pain, the self-hatred, the confusion, the anxiety, each monstrous and immense. Pulling a shiny blade up my pale arm figured perfectly then as the next, logical step. A door I'd never come to before swung open in my mind. Through the doorway was deep space, a black starless vacuum, light years away from everyone I'd ever known. It was my cold, lonely death. I stared at it. I needed only step over the threshold and tip through.

I writhed all night. My body was bone dry. I thought about the butcher knives in the kitchen until morning. They made small, squeaking noises in my mind. When the boy left for work, I clawed my way back into the bed and fell asleep, both anticipating and dreading his return later that day. And it was this ambivalence—fearing he would leave me, fearing he would stay—that felt like my biggest betrayal of all.

\* \* \*

Soon after the night on the bedroom floor, the boy decided he needed professional help and announced he was sending himself to an addiction treatment center all the way across the country in Arizona. Already familiar with the treatment world, he considered what was happening between us was dire and gave me a copy of *Facing Love Addiction,* a book which I would read and re-read, poring over each word in "Love Addicts and Their Relationships" and "The Progressive Stages of Love Addiction." I scrawled obsessively in the margins: "objectifying myself," "evil rescuer???," yes," "hello!?" and "me, me, me." On page 11 I underlined, highlighted, and starred, "We may decide we want to stop using the substance of doing the compulsive behavior only to find that we cannot."

The book talked a lot about positive and negative intensity, unhealthy boundaries, and simultaneous fears of both intimacy and abandonment. It had pie charts and diagrams and numbered lists which neatly laid out how love addiction worked and its progressive stages: increasing tolerance of inappropriate behavior from another, greater dependence on the person, decrease in self-care, disconnection from feelings, and a sense of being trapped.

What was happening between me and the boy was finally explainable, something that could be defined, parsed, analyzed, and then diagrammed. It all seemed so scientific, as if resolving the emotional turmoil of what we'd been experiencing was as easy as applying the scientific method. I wanted to believe what we had was fixable, whether by therapy or prescription or sheer force of will. I wanted to believe that if I could just figure out some key connection, finally chart the pathology of our relationship, I would finally be able to save it. I went online and found a facility that was also in Arizona, just an hour away from where he would be.

We boarded the same flight from DC to Phoenix and then took turns crying for the next 1500 miles. The concerned flight attendant kept offering us iced drinks, and my shoulder was wet and dark by the time we began our descent into the desert, a landscape like Mars with red dust and black rock mountains, white light frying everything that tried to live. I boarded a white van, crying. He stood outside my window, crying. We matched palms through the glass in between.

After the van pulled away, I put on my headphones and fell asleep to *I Always Thought That I'd See You Again*, dreamt about the boy's pale face, then woke up in a supermarket parking lot where a tough woman from the rehab center waited for me on a bench. She started right in with talk about being clean and sober, as she loaded my suitcase into her SUV. I tried to explain I was here because of my boyfriend, but she seemed to think it was all the same thing.

I arrived at the center exhausted, toting my oversized suitcase, fifteen pounds underweight with dark circles under my eyes. Three women, my apartment mates, were watching TV in the living room, and one looked up and asked me, "So what are you here for?"

"Um, I'm depressed. And, you know, stuff with my family. Maybe alcohol. Love addiction?" I offered meekly. "What about you?"

"Alcohol," she said. "Drugs. Abuse issues. Eating disorders. Codependency. Depression. Anxiety. PTSD. OCD. Everything."

And she was nothing compared to my roommate, whose mom had been murdered, whose dad had died when she was eighteen, and who, before the age of twenty, had been a stripper and a meth addict. Yet here I was at the same place, and all I could really say in response to anyone who asked why was, "I really miss my boyfriend."

In addition to group therapy, we were required to attend a daily twelve-step meeting. I tried Alcoholics Anonymous and Narcotics Anonymous but couldn't connect with people who talked about booze and drugs when all I wanted to talk about was the boy who I loved and missed and wanted to be with, I don't care what anyone says, I love him and I always will. So I stuck to SLAA meetings: Sex and Love Addicts Anonymous.

These meetings were co-ed. Had I been in a different state of mind, I no doubt would have gone the way of many of my treatment center compatriots by making cow eyes at the guys across the room and eventually starting a clandestine romance that would ultimately get me kicked out of treatment. Instead, I actually sat and listened. I heard from fellow addicts outlandish stories of vitriolic romances, suicidal tendencies, obsessive thoughts. Crazy, I thought, until I considered how similar their stories were to my own.

* * *

I wasn't allowed to speak with the boy during my first month of treatment. Imagine, then, my psychotic delight when I returned to my apartment one afternoon at the end of that month to find his voice cooing from the answering machine: "It's me, your boyfriend." These words might as well have been high-grade heroin. I wouldn't be surprised if my pupils dilated. I re-played it once, twice, ten times in a euphoric trance.

"Are you ever going to delete that thing?" my roommate asked days later.

I cradled the answering machine to my ear and hit Play yet again. She shook her head.

The reason for his call was to invite me to his treatment center for our very own family week. His undying love for me was confirmed when I discovered I got a week alone with him, no other family, just us. I imagined our teary reunion, big-hearted acknowledgements of wrongdoing, non-accusatory "I" statements.

Thursday of that week was our ten month anniversary, and I had balloons sent to the center, a surprise.

This was also the day of our special meeting. The boy and I sat across from each other in a room with the blinds drawn. My therapist who had been assigned to me for the week was on my left. The boy's therapist was on my right. She was the woman who'd written the book on love addiction, the one I'd underlined and starred and annotated, partially memorized, taken to heart. She had short, curled hair, so blonde it was almost white. Her eyes were dark and cold and, when she smiled, they stayed that way.

The boy started talking, saying how things had been hard, how being my boyfriend had made him sick, how worrying about me all the time was heavy, an awful weight. He checked his notebook, splayed open on his lap, then continued, talked about the pills he'd been taking, way too many, then talked about his ex-girlfriend in Japan, the one he said he'd broken up with ten months ago, talked about how he'd actually never broken up with her, how they'd still been talking for all these months. I nodded, nodded, trying to smile. I am such an understanding girlfriend. Nod. I am forgiving. Nod nod. I kept trying to hold my face in one position, to demonstrate how level-headed I was, how understanding. I could remember all the times he'd talked with her on the phone in front of me. A friend, he'd said, followed by indistinguishable conversations in Japanese. I didn't even care. I didn't. I would forgive him absolutely everything because that's how healthy I'd grown. I was better. I was different. I was finally who he wanted me to be.

He started talking again, about how I looked at guys, how I talked with them, my drinking, the kind of girl he thought I was. It all blurred together, what he was saying in the cool, dark room, until he reached the end, about how he couldn't be with someone he didn't trust, and how he didn't trust me.

He paused and I looked at him, smiling and nodding. What next? Perhaps something about how now he was learning how to trust me since I was in rehab and working so hard to change. I waited. Instead, my therapist looked at me, eyebrows raised.

"Do you understand what he's saying?" he asked.

"He doesn't trust me," I said.

"Yes. And he can't be with you. Do you understand?"

I felt a cog, rusty and unoiled, wrench and then turn in my head. I opened my mouth and nothing came out. Tears and sweat spontaneously glossed my face.

"She's going to puke," the boy said, and his therapist moved a plastic trashcan beside my chair.

"These are the painful consequences of your actions," she said, looking me in the eyes. I hyperventilated and lowered my head between my knees, just above the trashcan. I sobbed, spewing strings of incoherence, hiccupping and coughing, gagging and then muttering profanity-laced assaults.

"What about what he did?" I wanted to know. "What the fuck about him?"

"You should be thankful to him for helping you get here," his therapist said to me evenly.

"Fuck off," I told her. I hated her almost more than him, her stupid book I'd studied to no avail, her defense of him, this man, when I was a woman, like her, when she should have been on my side. I looked at the boy, desperate for some sign this was all a big mistake. He merely stared at his palms, then at me, blankly.

"Seriously?" I said to him, doubled-over, holding my stomach. I couldn't breathe. "You're seriously doing this?"

He nodded.

"Well, fuck all of you," I said, slouching back in my chair. "Are we done?"

"Do you have anything you want to say?" my therapist asked.

I looked at this hunched boy across from me, this boy who I had been willing to do anything for, this stupid, beautiful boy. I couldn't say anything. I sobbed and sobbed and sobbed.

"You need to pull yourself together, Rachel," his therapist said. "You need to be in your adult self."

I breathed deeply, then gagged into the trash can.

Ten minutes later, I tried to participate in our next scheduled group therapy session, but my crying was distracting everyone, so I slammed out of the room and onto the lawn, where the greenness and sun and sound of the birds all seemed like pointed attacks. I raged through the hallways slamming doors and spewing profanity, then collapsed into fits of malevolent despair only to be ushered to various shady cots throughout the facility. I refused to wear shoes. I insulted all who implored me to calm down. Back at the motel where I was staying, I vomited my spaghetti lunch and then endured a night of cold sweats and endless half-dream delirium in the blue light of late night TV. I woke up with a biting headache and developed an embarrassing twitch.

The next morning, I said goodbye to the boy in the treatment center parking lot.

"I got your balloons," he said. "Right after we broke up. It was horrible."

"Good," I said. "I want you to feel horrible."

"Don't," he said, his hands resting on my shoulders.

"I love you," I said, and we clutched each other. I couldn't stop crying. "I love you. Why are you doing this?"

He shook his head. I could feel the tiredness radiating from both of us, a demoralized exhaustion, as if everything alive had been taken from us, as if we might lay down that night and sleep for years.

"It's what's best," he said into my ear, his nose wet with tears. I hated him so much that I loved him. I believed one day, maybe in a year, maybe ten, we'd be back together. I had to believe this because otherwise I never would have left that parking lot, pulling away from him as he waved weakly, watching him in the rear view until he had disappeared, speeding back up the switchbacks of the mountain, crying, driving faster and faster away from him as the day faded away into peach and gold, lemon, bone, sky, dust.

*  *  *

Back at my treatment center, without the boy's approval or our ultimate reunion as motivation for my recovery, I was forced to consider how I might instead get better for my own sake. I started to do all those charmingly neurotic things you see in the movies about rehab: I took up kickboxing, crocheted an afghan the size of Rhode Island, and ate many, many cookies. I watched horrible reality dating shows religiously, got a job waitressing, developed a crush, and made plans to finish college. I listened to his message over and over—"It's me—your boyfriend...Your boyfriend...Your boyfriend..."—until one day when I finally, unceremoniously, erased it.

For a long time I blamed the boy for my life falling apart and felt victimized by him, our relationship, and my own backhanded desire. I tried to make sense of my seeming un-fixability, an amorphous and lingering sense of brokenness, and my diagnosis of love addict. I spent my twenties in and out of twelve-step programs, dabbling in homeopathy and acupuncture, breath work, vegetarianism, yoga, therapy, therapy, therapy. And, of course, there were men, men with potential only I could see, men who I tried to love into better, happier, more successful iterations of themselves. If I couldn't fix myself, I figured, might as well try my best to jimmy-rig someone else back together.

None of this worked. Or, I should say, none of it worked in the way I had been hoping. Real change, of course, happened slowly, so slowly it didn't seem to be happening at all. Six years after rehab, I moved back to the Arizona desert to attend graduate school and again found myself amidst perplexed saguaros, swooning from loneliness and a recent break-up, this time with a kind man who I just couldn't be with. Those first few months were some of the hardest since treatment, and I wondered how, after so much time, I could be back in the same desolate place feeling much the same way.

The nights in Tucson were long and hot, the heat unrelenting even at 3 A.M. I spent hours out on my patio, staring at the old pairs of shoes slung up on the electric lines in the alley, thinking and thinking. What's wrong with me, I wanted to know as I smoked cigarettes and tied my hair up on top of my head. I watched the shadows of the bushes against the stucco walls.

An old woman with an old dog lived next door. I complained about the dog's barking so she put a shock collar on it and, at night, when the dog tried to bark, all that came out was a terrible, pained squawk. I listened to this through my bedroom window, regret ballooning inside me until there was no hope for sleep. In the darkness, I went to the fence and scratched the dog's ears to apologize. I wish I could have taken it all back. There was an old blue boat in the backyard, a big thing with a tall mast. Nights like that when I couldn't sleep, I took photos of it, long-exposure shots that came out yellow and shadowy.

The sky spread wide and dark and full of clouds. I pointed my camera upward and opened the shutter and wondered what would be there when the eye of the camera shut, what would remain. The stars up there, the galaxies—most of them no longer existed, their light an expression of what had once been, traveling for so long, across inconceivable lengths of time and space, it outlived the body that had created it. Once the photos developed, I saw what was

really there: a darkly violet sky with bleached white clouds.
No stars, no lost galaxies. It was frightening and gorgeous.
It almost looked like day.

# SAYONARA MARIJUANA MON AMOUR

## Chase Twichell

In the mornings black tea uplifts me,
and at night I invite wine to tell
its stories in my mouth. If I nap,
a different mind awakes than the one
that lay down and dreamed of swimming.
Both dreaming and swimming alter consciousness.
So do zazen, weeding, and sex.
Marijuana makes me self and
unself-conscious simultaneously,
like playing with dogs.
The first time I got high, we gathered
at the monument in East Rock Park.
I read the plaque to the Union Dead.
Moving from one mind to another
was familiar to me, as was the sensation
of watching myself, as if the dead and I
were the audience, and my friends
were real, and in the world.
As a kid I believed that the dead
lay inside the monuments,
that each monument was a tomb,
proof of death one old stone wall away,
the same distance as the friends.
Whatever it is in me that was born striving
was also born craving and clinging.
Once, when I'd drunk too much wine,
the dogs and I stood in the snowy yard,

their wet black nostrils working,
drawing in scents from a realm
unknown to me. I looked up at the great
dust-light of stars, and there was my question
spelled out for me, in plain sight.
But *whose* question was it?
I must not want to be fully enlightened,
since I do not devote myself entirely to it.
I like distraction. Whenever I'm distracted,
a new room appears for my perusal,
or an ocean, or a neighborhood lit
by childhood's untrustworthy flashlights,
half dreamed-up, half memory.
Or lit by the alpenglow or northern lights,
under the constellation Not Here Not Now,
where I have wasted most of my life.

I often berate myself, renew my vows,
forsake all toys, recite the Gatha of Atonement.
I pledge austerity; I scorn squander.
*No* (imaginary teacher talking), *that misses it.*
*Toys are neither right nor wrong.*

When I wonder which of these nights
will be the night I renounce it,
the spank in the intake surprises me again,
and I return its resinous kiss.
It tastes of every mouth that ever
stopped kissing me to ask me
what consciousness was (very few,
but those are the ones I remember).

# THE BEEP

## Anna David

The first time I got rip-roaring drunk, I'd just had a vicious fight with my parents. I don't remember what the fight was about—I only remember the viciousness of it. Tears were involved. Both parents were involved—which was notable only because my father was gone so much of the time that parental battles tended to be one-on-one affairs. I wish I could remember what we were fighting about that night. It couldn't have been my low SAT scores because I was only a freshman in high school at the time. It couldn't have been about Dad getting busted for embezzlement because that didn't happen until my junior year and we didn't fight about that or even really talk about it at all.

I remember that we fought because I remember sitting in my bedroom afterwards and looking at myself in my full-length mirror—my blotchy face, my puffy eyes, tears still streaming out of them—and thinking that I was going to have to call my friend and explain that I couldn't go into the city to the party she'd invited me to.

We lived in Marin, a suburb outside of San Francisco, and going into the city was something special—not only were the people more sophisticated (at the time, this translated into more appealing boys) but also if we were going into the city, that meant we were spending the night. Which meant we could get rip roaring drunk.

Since we were freshmen, we didn't have our licenses yet so I can't recall who drove us in. A clueless parent, believing whatever lie we were perpetuating about the movie we were going to watch or the test we were going to study for? An older friend? God knows. Ironically, what I remember best about that night is the part that I shouldn't remember—the rip-roaring drunk part. I remember it so well because I couldn't believe that I could go from feeling as despondent as I did to not just rip-roaring drunk but an excellent kind of rip-roaring drunk.

I don't remember how I went from planning to cancel to going to the party. What I recall was my shock over the power that booze had: it could transform a too-painful-to-be-endured experience into an unpleasant memory, a fight over something not even worth remembering. I'd suddenly found a solution to pain—and an instant solution at that. Alcohol could upend every sliver of pain, turn agony into joy. It was the greatest discovery of my life.

\* \* \*

I don't remember the first time I got depressed. Or actually I might. I have a memory of being five and feeling sad while in the waiting room of my parents' marriage counselor but I think it may be one of those fake memories—something I heard about and made up a story around. Or maybe it is real. If it's real, I remember that my mom took me to Kentucky Fried Chicken right before and an older boy looked at me at the shopping center afterwards in a way that made me uncomfortable. But mostly I remember sitting in my parents' marriage counselor's waiting room, surrounded by toys (did a lot of people bring their kids to wait outside? Why were there so many toys?) thinking that I really didn't believe my parents should be married. Where was my brother? Why wasn't I home with a babysitter? How could I have been five and still understand the concept of a marriage counselor, let alone the concept that my parents shouldn't be married? These are more questions for the unanswerable bin.

\* \* \*

I don't remember when depression became a semi-regular part of my life. These things can change the longer you have to reflect on them but as I still see it, I was a pretty happy kid. My dad suffered from depression. My grandmother on my mom's side had been depressed. But I didn't think I was. When I was younger, if I ever had a temper tantrum—and, as a late bloomer, I had these well into adulthood—my dad would wave one of his Lithium pills at me. "You need this," he'd say. "You have a problem, just like me. It's you and me against the world."

The last thing in the world I wanted was to be just like him. "No." I'd say. "You need that shit. I don't."

At a certain point, I did. Not Lithium but an array of different anti-depressants. There was a Prozac phase and a longer Paxil one but neither were terribly effective—the Prozac because, the shrink and I determined, that drug just didn't work for me, and the Paxil because by the time I started taking it, the cocaine I was also taking was rendering whatever serotonin raising the poor, defenseless SSRI was attempting utterly useless.

\* \* \*

I was not someone who should have liked cocaine. I've always been very energetic, very jittery, very wired. If I was going to do a drug with enthusiasm, it should have been pot or acid or mushrooms or even Ecstasy. But pot just made me paranoid that no one understood what it was I was trying to say—a fear exacerbated by the fact that when I was high, I made almost no sense so no one did understand what I was trying to say. Mushrooms and Ecstasy were okay but didn't give me that kick. And I had as much interest in acid as I did in bathing in hot wax: expanding my mind so that I could go deeper into myself, have profound realizations and maybe imagine some spiders? Ugh! I was born far deeper into myself than I ever wanted to be. I wanted the opposite. I wanted out.

Cocaine got me out. It made me the me I'd always wanted to be: me, but euphoric. Everything, from whatever cigarette I happened to be smoking to whatever fact I happened to be expounding on (and, in the initial years, I expounded on a lot of facts), excited me. Cocaine made me fall in love with myself—a state unimagined during all those years of subconscious yet crippling self-recrimination. While falling in love with myself surely made me annoying company, this wasn't a problem in the beginning since I was surrounded by many others who were having similar self love affairs and we were all happy to co-exist together. It can be depressing when everyone around you is in love—unless you, too, are in the same boat. In those early days, the group of us could remain confident that we all had someone to love and were also loved back.

The center, of course, could not hold.

People who are utterly convinced of their own brilliance can become tiresome, particularly if they're competing with your cocaine-addled brain for airtime. No, you find yourself wanting to say, the idea of starting a website where we give people financial advice based on their astrological signs is not a good one. No, you realize, you don't think the group of you should consider starting a band, seeing as none of you play instruments or sing. These people, you suddenly realize, are losers.

You don't think of yourself as a loser at this point. At least, you're doing your best not to.

\* \* \*

I'm amazed it took me as long as it did to start using coke by myself. But once I started, I never looked back. True, there were those times—days, weeks, months or years, I'm really not sure—where I was dancing that line of doing drugs alone while still attempting to socialize with others. It was like *Being John Malkovich*—the elevator had stopped at a floor that didn't really exist and I was stuck there: sane enough to still have people around yet crazy enough to be doing cocaine without telling them.

This also marked the official point when cocaine turned on me, transitioning from energy-giver to energy-zapper.

I'd be out, with people, and suddenly unable to talk to them because I'd be too consumed with thoughts about how whoever I was trying to talk to surely knew I was high and clearly thought I was a really fucked up person to be high by myself and come to think of it, that person was completely right. All the love cocaine had made me feel for myself had turned to hate and there was no way to break up. I couldn't toss my belongings out a window in a rage, change my cell phone number to cut off contact, file a restraining order. I was stuck with me.

And the only way to deal with that harsh reality was to sneak off to do more cocaine by myself while worrying obsessively about who was seeing me and what they were thinking. Cocaine made me into a celebrity in my own mind, and all the other inhabitants of my world employees of TMZ—ever hoping to catch me with rolled-up dollar bill in hand, white powder on face, so they could inform the world of my indiscretions.

*  *  *

The first time I stayed up by myself all night, high, I wrote a brilliant television spec script.

It was for *3rd Rock From The Sun*, a show I'd never seen, but no matter. I was writing the Hollywood way—by studying other people's scripts in the hopes of mimicking one enough while also injecting enough of myself into it for my words to rise from the bottom of the slush pile to the top.

I really hated the scripts I'd read for *3rd Rock From the Sun*, but no matter. After pouring cocaine onto the framed print my mom had given me, slicing it into lines and ingesting a few in the name of getting my creative juices flowing, I suddenly saw the hidden brilliance of *3rd Rock*.

Which led me to come up with a genius idea for an episode.
Which led to me writing the genius episode that night.

Initially, it was surprising when the birds started chirping
and I heard my neighbor leave for work. People who do
coke in L.A., I would come to learn, are greeted each
morning by birds creating a cacophony of cheer so far from
the state of mind of the average cocaine user at that time of
the morning that somehow they make suicide sound like a
reasonable escape. But this came later. That morning, after
completing my brilliant spec script, the birds sounded
lovely—like a harbinger of joyous news to come. Television
writing jobs. Riches. New friends. Happiness. If I needed
cocaine to help make that happen, I remember reasoning, so
be it.

Alas, it was not to be. My *3rd Rock* spec script was not
decreed the paean of brilliance I'd been sure it would be. (I
still maintain that it's a damn fine effort.) But, even worse,
my writing system—do two lines to get the creative juices
flowing followed by two lines every twenty minutes or so
for the following eight to fourteen hours in order to keep
the flow happening—became instantly ineffective.

The next time I sat down to write, I couldn't do it. And
by "it", I mean move. Cocaine, the drug that had once
made me ebullient, transforming every lampshade into a
potential hat and keeping the party going all night long,
betrayed me even further. It made me unable to do anything
but sit in front of my computer and shake.

I'd be crouched there, thinking about how badly I had to
pee, really wanting to get up and go to the bathroom. But
I'd be too jittery to stand up. Or too frightened. So I'd just
stay there and shake. I was capable of some movements: I
could wipe my nose and chain smoke and even occasionally
rise to peer out the window at the neighbors—a composer
and his wife, do-gooders who I was convinced spied on me
with binoculars.

One movement I could not make, alas, involved tapping
keys on the keyboard. I'd stare at the screen, at the Great

American Screenplay I'd convinced myself I was writing. And I'd have a lot of ideas for how to make it better. Too many of them, alas. I'd want to try one but there was the shaking to contend with and just the fact that I couldn't seem to find a way to tap the letters out. Still, I'll say one thing for me: I never gave up. I never said, "Gosh, this writing while wired thing isn't working out. Maybe I should watch a movie." I just stayed there and kept trying.

The worst part of it all, as I saw it, was the way my computer worked. If you didn't hit a key for sixty seconds, a box would pop onto the screen asking if you wanted to save. The question would be accompanied by a beep. Now I don't know how loud a beep it was—how loud I would consider it today—but I know this: in the state I was in, that noise sounded like a megaphone inside a microphone inside my ear. And so I lived in fear of the beep. It somehow symbolized just how bad things were. If I could avoid the beep, I somehow thought, that meant everything was okay.

I couldn't avoid the beep.

I'd sit there, huddled, telling myself to just hit a key—any key!—so I could buy myself some time. But there was a disconnect between my brain and my hand and it wouldn't happen. I'd be in fearful anticipation, thinking, "Do something or the beep will come…the beep is coming…Dear God, it's getting closer…Do something now!" But nothing would happen and then—

BEEP!

I'd nearly jump out of my skin, every time. And then I'd spend the next fifty-nine seconds or so trying to avoid the next beep, and miss it.

\* \* \*

I'm not sure how long it took me to realize I was depressed. I'd been down for so long that I forgot what not feeling down felt like. The fact that I had a propensity for depression, that depression was in my family, was in my blood, and that depressants like alcohol and cocaine were surely exacerbating that, wasn't something I could afford to think about. I needed cocaine—and though I told myself I didn't need alcohol, I had no interest in giving it up, either. I needed cocaine even though it had gotten to the point where I'd buy it, flush it in a fit of shame, and then call my dealer for more. I needed it when it left me living in fear of a beep I couldn't escape.

It began to dawn on me that my relationship with cocaine was less than healthy. I had, I could admit, an issue with it. I don't think I was comfortable using the word "addiction." But I knew that if I had the drug on me, I couldn't stop ingesting it until the supply was drained and I had the additional problem of not being able to resist calling my dealer to replenish. I knew what had to be done.

I quit cocaine. It wasn't easy but I did it.

Of course, I needed some comfort through this deprivation, so I allowed myself to drink. And, in fact, I drank quite a bit because my alcohol consumption had increased with all the cocaine use—only because I needed it to come down—and what with giving up coke and everything, I didn't see why I should make myself suffer needlessly by trying to tone down the drinking.

A month passed. And I reasoned that no one who has an issue with cocaine gives up the drug for an entire thirty days.

And so I went back to using it.

I did the quitting-for-a-month thing a few more times. The experiments had variations: during one, a guy I was dating, a pill popper, told me he thought I had a problem so I asked another guy I'd dated to take me to a twelve-step meeting. God, I hated it. The people I met there all insisted that there was no way I could have an issue with cocaine but not with alcohol, even when I tried explaining how little I enjoyed drinking anymore. But, I reasoned, I could go along with their program. I could be sober.

I made it ten days.

Ten days where I was regularly taking the Vicodin that my then-boyfriend agreed to share. After ten days, I'd had enough. *Fuck sobriety*, I said, really believing I'd been sober.

The very last time I quit cocaine but continued to drink, I wanted to die. And not just in the passive way I'd been wanting to die the previous few years. I was really there. I understood that drugs and alcohol were doing this to me but I was certain I couldn't live without them. I didn't have the courage to go get razors or swallow pills so I considered driving my car into oncoming traffic. I never considered the fact that if I drove my car into oncoming traffic, I could hurt or kill someone else.

Then it occurred to me that getting sober might be better than dying. I figured it probably wasn't but reasoned that I could give the sobriety thing a try and if it turned out I was right—that it, in fact, was worse—I could always reconsider the whole dying thing.

That was almost ten and-a-half years ago and I haven't reconsidered it yet. This doesn't mean that I now see sunshine and rainbows where I once only saw darkness and jittery nights. I still experience depression—just not nearly as often as I used to and I almost always understand that it's going to pass. I still, occasionally, fight with my parents—who, as it turns out, are no longer married—but I never get hysterical about it. Essentially, I have a real life— one filled with pain and hope and panic and peace and, at times, the instant pain relief and euphoria that alcohol and then cocaine once gave me. I'm still a writer, but now I actually do it. My fingers don't hover over the keyboard, unable to move.

I haven't heard The Beep in over a decade. Luckily, I still remember exactly how it sounds.

# IF THERE'S A GOD...

## Gregory Orr

If there's a god of amphetamine, he's also the god of wrecked lives, and it's only he who can explain how my doctor father, with the gift of healing strangers and patients alike, left so many intimate dead in his wake.

If there's a god of amphetamine, he's also the god of recklessness, and I ask him to answer.

He's the god of thrills, the god of boys riding bikes down steep hills with their hands over their heads.

He's the god of holy and unholy chance, the god of soldiers crossing a field and to the right of you a man falls dead and to the left also and you are still standing.

If there's a god of amphetamine, he's the god of diet pills, who is the god of the fifties housewife who vacuums all day and whose bathroom is spotless and now it is evening as she sits alone in the kitchen, polishing her chains.

He's the god of the rampant mind and the god of my father's long monologues by moonlight in the dark car driving over the dusty roads.

He's the god of tiny, manic orderings in the midst of chaos, the god of elaborate charts where Greg will do this chore on Monday and a different one on Tuesday and all the brothers are there on the chart and all the chores and all the days of the week in a miniscule script no one can read.

If there's a god of amphetamine, my father was his hopped-up acolyte who leapt out of bed one afternoon to chase a mouse through the house, shouting, firing his .38

repeatedly at the tiny beast scurrying along the wall while Jon wailed for help from the next room.

If there's a god of amphetamine, he's the god of subtle carnage and dubious gifts who lives in each small pill tasting of electricity and dust.

If there's a god of amphetamine, my father was its high priest, praising it, preaching its gospel, lifting it like a host and intoning: "Here in my hand is the mystery: a god alive inside a tiny tablet. He is a high god, a god of highs—he eats the heart to juice the brain and mocks the havoc he makes, laughing at all who stumble. Put out your tongue and receive it."

# INSTRUCTIONS ON THE USE OF ALCOHOL

## James Brown

### *I*

You're young, maybe nine or ten, and your parents are throwing a party. All the adults are laughing and talking too loudly, just in general having a good time, and you put two-and-two together. What makes them happy comes out of those bottles on the kitchen counter. The brown ones, you learn soon enough, contain whiskey and scotch. The clear ones hold vodka and gin and that odd shaped bottle with the long neck, something called *Midori*, contains a thick syrupy green liquid. That's the one that intrigues you most, and when the adults aren't looking you pour yourself a glass. You sneak it into our room. You lock the door. At first you sniff at it, the green liquid, and because it doesn't smell so good you pinch your nostrils shut before you take a swallow.

It burns the back of your throat. It makes your eyes water. You shake your head violently, and for a few minutes, until the alcohol takes effect, you can't understand how anyone in their right mind could drink this stuff. But then a tingling sensation begins to spread through your chest, your face is warm and flushed, and you're suddenly light-headed. You feel good. In fact, you feel great, and now you understand why it's worth braving the foul taste, the burn in your throat and the watery eyes. It's as if you've made a major discovery, a real inroad to the secret of a good life, and it only makes sense that if one drink has this effect on you that a second will make you feel even better.

You finish the glass and sneak another. You repeat this action several more times.

The party ends around midnight but you wouldn't know it because you're deathly ill. Because you've lost all that sugary green liqueur along with dinner and hors d'oeuvres before you promptly passed out in bed. In the morning, you wake with a miserable headache. Your mouth is so dry you can hardly swallow, you're still nauseous, too, and right then and there you vow never again to so much as look at a bottle of Midori. But what the seasoned drunk knows that the apprentice does not is that those of us predisposed to alcoholism are hardwired to quickly forget our unfortunate drinking experiences. In a day or two all you remember is how good the liquor made you feel, and when you go over to a relative's house for dinner that following weekend you find yourself sneaking into the kitchen again. You open the cupboard with the colorful bottles, and instead of the green stuff this time, because there is no green stuff in this household, you choose the liquid in the clear bottle with that weird Russian name of *Stolichnaya*, or simply Stoli, as you learn to call it many years later, sidling up to the bar. This brand burns more than the Midori but it also packs a faster, more powerful punch, and that's exactly what you're after. Drunk, you find yourself smarter and funnier and stronger and braver and even better-looking. For the budding alcoholic, booze seems to do more for you than it does others, and your only regret, at least to date, is that you didn't come across this miracle potion sooner.

## II

You're older now, maybe fifteen or sixteen, and by no stretch of the word would anyone outside of an uptight substance abuse counselor consider you a problem drinker, let alone alcoholic. Liquor has actually lost some of its initial luster, and you rarely sneak drinks anymore, say, only once or twice a week. What currently interests you is marijuana and the intrigue that surrounds it. Booze just isn't as cool, and besides you like the subterfuge, the cloak-and-dagger melodrama of doing something forbidden. Breaking the law is a high in itself, and just as importantly it befits the rebel image of your teenage years. You enjoy scoring the weed behind the bleachers at your high school almost as much as you do smoking it. You enjoy showing off to your friends how well you can roll a joint, and because the dope world has its own language, all the slang and clever code words, you feel special when you speak it. Tough. Streetwise. And don't for a minute believe all those lies you hear about marijuana being addicting. About how it damages the brain. If you want proof, just ask someone who's been smoking it daily for twenty years, but ask him slowly and be prepared to repeat yourself.

Then one day you try to connect with that kid behind the bleachers, the guy with all the Bob Marley stickers on his notebook, and it isn't happening.

"It's bone-dry out there," he says. "Fucking drought season, man."

Apparently some big bust went down in Humboldt County where they grow some of the world's best sensimilla and now everyone's hoarding what they have and scrambling to find more. But he does have something else, if you're interested, this stuff he calls blow—a white powder you put up your nose. "It's good shit," he tells you. "Eighty percent pure." Since you've been such a loyal customer, he's willing to cut you a deal, a gram for fifty bucks, or an eight-ball, three and a half grams, for a hundred and twenty. It's too good to pass up, especially since there's no weed around, and there's also a party this weekend where you'd look pretty cool laying out some lines of coke in the bathroom for a few select friends. Or that girl you like. With some good dope and a little luck, you might even get laid. Blow, you've been told, is something of an aphrodisiac.

You enjoy making the buy, even more so now, because the stakes are higher with narcotics, the penalties worse if you're caught. You enjoy the preparations, carefully chopping the crystals with a shiny razor blade, drawing out neat even lines and scraping the bag, or bindle, for every last particle. And as it happens with your first drink, so it is with the coke. It makes you feel great. It makes you stronger and smarter and braver and even better looking. All your fears and insecurities fall to the wayside when you're wired and you dismiss those lies you've heard about coke being addicting. Getting hooked is for weaklings, the idiots who can't control themselves, those losers who end up broke and penniless, wandering the streets at night like zombies, like the walking dead. You'll never be one of them, though you can see how the stuff might drain your bank account, since the rush is so short, and the more you use, the more it takes to get the same high. Where a couple of grams used to last you a week, now you're lucky if you can stretch that amount a full day. For the budding addict, the supply is never enough, but your only regret, at least to date, is that you didn't come across this miracle powder sooner.

## III

You survive your teenage years. You even make it through college drinking and drugging whenever you get a chance, which is about every other night, with all stops pulled on the weekends. At this point you're in your late twenties and still have no idea that you might have a slight problem. Who, after all, doesn't like to party? Who, after all, doesn't deserve a couple of drinks at the end of a hard day? A joint now and then never killed anybody, either. The same goes for a few lines of coke, a hit of Ecstasy now and then, or LSD, and a little heroin is actually a good thing if you're strung out on speed and need to settle your nerves.

Imagine how boring life would be if you had to live it straight twenty-four seven. Imagine how boring you'd be as a person if you couldn't get a little loose, a little crazy from time to time. The whole idea is to escape our dull existence, to find some amusement, some relief from the monotony of the day-to-day grind. This is how you rationalize it, anyway, and through the years you become very good at it.

If you have a rough day, it's reason to drink. If you had a good one, it's reason to celebrate. And if you get into it with your wife, because somewhere in this chemical fog you fall in love and marry, that is definitely grounds for storming out of the house and holding up in the neighborhood bar. Lately, this is the only place you seem to find any real peace, among men and women like yourself, the ones who don't judge you. So what if you like to drink yourself into a stupor. So what if you have a DUI or two. Half the people in this bar do, and like you they all chalk it up to the same thing, bad luck, being in the wrong place at the wrong time. You actually drive better now after a couple of drinks, because you're safer, you take fewer chances, because you don't want to get busted again. And furthermore, if anyone's complaining, your drinking hasn't caused you to miss a day of work in months. That you're so hung over or strung out and frequently have to go home after lunch doesn't count.

You just can't understand why your wife continues to nag or break down in tears. All the bills are paid. The kids are clothed and fed and you and she both drive newer cars. For a real drunk, you think, for a real junkie, none of this would be possible. You'd have already lost it all or never made it to begin with. But whether you know it or not, and you don't, things are changing deep inside you and have been for some time: hormones, genes, brain chemistry, all of it adapts to the alcohol and drugs you continually dump into your body. The cells habituate. The cells literally mutate to accommodate your cravings and now they crave, too. Now your addiction has more to do with physiology than psychology. Now it's the body that robs the mind of its power to choose, and it's not long before you'll wish you never came across that miracle potion, those powders and pills.

## IV

Add a few years to this story and you're in your thirties, still going strong. God knows what happened to your old college buddies who used to match you shot for shot, line for line. They can't keep up with you anymore and not a single one even wants to try. How they just turned their back on you and the partying life, simply because they landed good jobs and married and had kids, you can't understand. What you think has been your dirty little secret for years has in fact been no secret at all to anyone who's ever made the mistake of loving or caring about you.

"It's time to grow up," one says, when you call him late at night, drunk out of your mind.

Grow up, you think. Sure. Your friends have sold out to the doldrums of suburban middle age. The truth is, you are and always have been tougher than them, blessed from the beginning with an iron constitution. A special ability to tolerate alcohol and whatever other poisons you consume. What you don't realize, however, is that this high tolerance is no gift but a liability, another sign and symptom of your addiction. And oddly enough, as you continue along this ever narrowing path, your tolerance will work exactly in the reverse, at least for the alcohol: where before it took ten drinks to get you reasonably drunk, now five will have you stumbling.

If you're not quite to this point yet, you're close. Your liver is enlarged. Your doctor has warned you, as has your boss for all the days of work you've been missing lately, assuming she hasn't already fired you. As for your marriage, it's in ruins, and you're up to your neck in debt. It makes you cringe to think of the thousands of dollars you've put up your nose or slapped down on the bar. The shame and guilt just compels you to drink more, and to start earlier, sometimes first thing in the morning if only to quell the horrible hangover from imbibing too heavily the night before.

Hair of the dog.

That's the cure, and since you're always worn out, since you're not getting any younger, you need a little bump - compliments of methamphetamine - to get you through the long hard day. Crank is cheaper than blow and better fits your budget. Crank is also stronger than blow, seven times stronger on the central nervous system, and at night you absolutely have to drink if you hope to sleep at all. At this stage of your addiction, your drinking and using has little to do with pleasure, or even escape. From here on out, it's about maintenance. From here on out it's about feeding those mutated cells, fighting off the intense depression that follows a binge, and trying, to the best of your weakened abilities, to carry on the bare semblance of a life. You are teetering on the edge of becoming the very thing you most feared—another loser, another zombie, one of the walking dead who wander the streets late at night, nameless, lost and forgotten.

V

Believe it or not, you hobble along like this for a couple more years. Obviously you've lost your job by now, or more likely several jobs, and your wife has left you and taken the kids. You're at a cold, ugly place in your life, and there doesn't appear to be any way out, any hope or chance of going anywhere but down. Then something happens. It could be a number of things. A close brush with death. A tragedy in the family, say, another DUI, a bad car wreck, or just a realization one morning when you look in the mirror and barely recognize the man before you. Somewhere in this haze, between sobering up and getting wasted again, it finally dawns on you that maybe, just maybe, you might have a problem.

These moments, however, are fleeting, especially when you try to quit, and you'll try many times in the next several months, only to find that by noon, your hands are shaking so badly you can't hold a pen to sign your own name. Nausea quickly sets in, you sweat profusely, your head throbs, and you think to yourself: *What the fuck am I doing? Give me a drink. A line. A pill. Anything to stop the pain.* The cure is worse than the illness, and you're far less sick when you're drinking and using than when you attempt to stop. Inside of a day, you're back at square one, and you hate yourself, as you lift the bottle to your lips, as you split open the bindle of coke or crank or whatever you could get your hands on. You hate yourself because you made a promise not to drink or drug for one measly day, and here you are, loaded again.

You're weak.

You're pathetic. You consider killing yourself, since that's what you're doing anyway, albeit slowly, and you probably would if you didn't have kids. If you'd lost entirely your ability to love. Sometimes that is the only difference between life and death, and it surprises you, it takes you completely off-guard that anyone in your family, that any of your old friends still actually care about you. How is it that they see something in you that you can't see in yourself, something worth salvaging, when for the most part you've caused them nothing but disappointment, hurt and shame? But they do, and one day when you come home to your crummy little apartment, or motel room, if you've sunk that far, and find a half dozen friends and family waiting for you, the same ones who wouldn't return your late night calls because they knew you'd only phoned to ask for money.

"You're sick," they tell you. "You need help. This is something you can't do alone."

In a matter of minutes, you're in the backseat of a friend or relative's car, being kidnapped really, whisked away to a hospital for junkies and drunks and where you remain for the next twenty-eight days.

That first week is a blur. To combat the onset of delirium tremens, the nurses give you round-the-clock doses of Valium, and because your blood pressure has rocketed off the charts, you're also administered Clonidine, a powerful antihypertensive, to further reduce the possibility of stroke. For some of us, the harder cases, detoxing from drugs and alcohol without medical supervision can and occasionally does kill. Fortunately this is not your case, and just days after you've weathered the worst of it, you wake up one morning actually feeling rested, actually sober for the first time in you don't know how many years, and it occurs to you right then and there that you might have a chance. That there is at least hope, even for a sorry bastard like yourself.

## VI

You're pushing forty now, a little beaten up for all the years of abuse, but for the most part you're still mentally and physically intact. You have no right to whine. No right to bitch. It's a minor miracle you're alive at all, and after a year or so of sobriety, you start to get back some of the things you lost. Maybe it's your job, if you have an understanding boss. Maybe it's visitation rights with your kids, if only for every other weekend. But don't count on patching it up with your wife. She's already moved on to another man, the guy who consoled her while you were out partying. The house, too, she's keeping that and everything in it. You feel so much guilt for destroying your marriage that you don't dare fight for what's yours.

Where every night you used to get whacked out of your head, now you attend A.A. meetings. You arrive early and make the coffee. You set out the donuts and fold-out chairs, and when things are underway and you're called on to speak, when you're asked to "share," you follow the A.A. protocol and first announce yourself as an alcoholic and addict. This is an important tenet of your sobriety: to remember always and forever that you are marked, that there is no cure for your affliction. One drink triggers the craving, and once the craving is on, you're off and running—next stop, the dope man's house. Beating the physical part of addiction is a cake-walk compared to silencing that voice in your head, the one that never goes away, telling you it's okay to have a drink, a line or a pill, because you've been clean and sober for a while. Because you can control it now. Compulsion is your soul mate, till death do you part, and your hold on sobriety is never more than tenuous.

But cheer up.

You've lost a lot but you've gained, too. If not wisdom, at least the return of your self-esteem. Your self-respect. And even though you've been condemned to a life sentence of A.A. meetings, even though you'll always be struggling with your addiction and may wind up back in rehab, at least for now, if only for this day, you are free of the miracle potions, powders and pills. If only for this day, you are not among the walking dead.

# ACKNOWLEDGEMENTS

Some of the material in this volume has appeared previously:

Frederick and Steven Barthelme, "Thrall" from *Double Down: Reflections on Gambling and Loss* by Frederick and Steven Barthelme. Copyright © 1999 by Frederick and Steven Barthelme. Reprinted by permission of Houghton Mifflin Harcourt Publishing Company. All rights reserved.

Kera Bolonik, "Lisa," first appeared in *Glamour* in April 2005 under the title, "Two Friends, One Suicide." Used by permission of the author.

James Brown, "Instructions on the Use of Alcohol," appeared under the title of, "How Some of Us Becomes Drunks and Junkies" and originally appeared in *Redivider: A Journal of New Literature.* Used with permission from Counterpoint Press, reprinted here from *This River: A Memoir.*

Margaret Bullitt-Jonas, "Putting Down the Duck," from *Holy Hunger: A Memoir of Desire* by Margaret Bullitt-Jonas, Copyright © 1998 by Margaret Bullitt-Jonas. Used by permission of Alfred A. Knopf, a division of Random House.

Maud Casey, "A Better Place to Live," was previously published in *Unholy Ghost: Writers on Depression*, edited by Nell Casey (HarperCollins, 2002). Used with permission.

Norton & Company, Inc. published by W.W. Norton & Company in 2001.

Chase Twichell, "Toys in the Attic," was previously published in *Unholy Ghost: Writers on Depression,* edited by Nell Casey (HarperCollins, 2002). Used with permission.

Chase Twichell, "Sayonara Marijuana Mon Amour," from *Horses Where the Answers Should Have Been: New and Selected Poems.* Copyright © 2010 by Chase Twichell. Reprinted with the permission of The Permissions Company, Inc. on behalf of Copper Canyon Press.

Rachel Yoder, "Night of the Violet Universe." Copyright © Rachel Yoder. An earlier version of this essay was originally published in *The New York Times,* June 11, 2006, under the title, "Strung Out on Love and Checked In for Treatment." Used with permission.

The editors would like to thank our publisher, Victor R. Volkman for his relentless support and belief in the project, Philip Lopate for suggesting the book title, and most importantly all the contributors for sharing their stories and poems of struggle and hope.

# APPENDIX

## SUPPORT GROUPS AND ORGANIZATIONS

### ALCOHOL AND DRUG ADDICTION

**Adult Children of Alcoholics**
(310) 534-1815
www.adultchildren.org

**Al-Anon/Alateen**
(757) 563-1600
www.al-anon.alateen.org

**Alcoholics Anonymous**
(212) 870-3400
www.aa.org

**Cocaine Addicts' Family Groups**
(520) 513-5088
www.co-anon.org

**Cocaine Anonymous**
(310) 559-5833
www.ca.org

**Crystal Meth Anonymous**
(213) 488-4455
www.crystalmeth.org

**Hazelden**
(800) 257-7810
www.hazelden.org

**Marijuana Anonymous**
(800) 766-6779
www.marijuana-anonymous.org

**Narcotics Anonymous**
(818) 773-9999
www.na.org

**National Association for Children of Alcoholics**
(888) 554-2627
www.nacoa.net

**National Council on Alcoholism and Drug Dependence**
(212) 269-7797
www.ncadd.org

**National Institute on Drug Abuse**
(301) 443-1124
www.nida.nih.gov

**National Youth Recovery Foundation**
(651) 773-8378
www.nationalyouthrecovery.com

**The Partnership**
(855) 378-4373
www.drugfree.org

**Sober Recovery**
www.soberrecovery.com

**Substance Abuse and Mental Health Services Administration (SAMHSA)**
(240) 276-2000
www.samhsa.gov

## EATING DISORDERS

**Anorexia Nervosa/Associated Disorders**
(847) 831-3438
www.anad.org

**Compulsive Eaters Anonymous**
(508) 891-2664
www.ceahowsci.com

**Mirasol**
(800) 520-1700
www.mirasol.net

**Overeaters Anonymous**
(505) 891-2664
www.oa.org

## GAMBLING

**Debtors Anonymous**
(310) 822-7250
www.debtorsanonymous.org

**Gamblers Anonymous**
(213) 386-8789
www.gamblersanonymous.org

## MENTAL HEALTH

**American Psychiatric Association**
(888) 357-7924
www.psych.org

**American Psychological Association**
(800) 374-2721
www.apa.org

**Association for Addiction Professionals**
(800) 548-0497
www.naadac.org

**Codependents Anonymous**
(888) 444-2359
www.coda.org

**Healthy Minds**
www.HealthyMinds.org

**Help Guide**
www.helpguide.org

**Mental Health America**
(703) 684-7722
www.nmha.org

**National Alliance on Mental Illness (NAMI)**
(800) 950-6264
www.nami.org

**National Association of Psychiatric Health Systems**
(202) 393-6700
www.naphs.org

**Workaholics Anonymous**
(510) 273-9253
www.workaholics-anonymous.org

## SELF-INJURY

**American Self-Harm Information Clearinghouse**
(206) 604-8963
www.selfinjury.org

**S.A.F.E. Alternatives**
(800) 366-8288
www.selfinjury.com

**Self Injury Foundation**
(888) 962-6774
www.selfinjuryfoundation.org

## SEX & LOVE ADDICTION

**Recovering Couples Anonymous**
(510) 663-2312
www.recovering-couples.org

**Sex Addicts Anonymous**
(800) 477-8191
www.sexaa.org

**Sex & Love Addicts Anonymous**
(210) 828-7900
www.slaafws.org

**Sexaholics Anonymous**
(800) 424-8777
www.sa.org

**Sexual Compulsives Anonymous**
(800) 977-HEAL
www.sca-recovery.org

# CONTRIBUTORS

JOHN AMEN is the author of three collections of poetry: *Christening the Dancer* (Uccelli Press 2003), *More of Me Disappears* (Cross-Cultural Communications 2005), and *At the Threshold of Alchemy* (Presa 2009). In addition, his work has appeared in numerous publications nationally and internationally. He has released two folk/folk rock CDs: *All I'll Never Need* (Cool Midget 2004) and *Ridiculous Empire* (2008). He is also an artist, working primarily with acrylics on canvas. Further information is available on his website: www.johnamen.com. Amen travels widely giving readings, doing musical performances, and conducting workshops. He founded and continues to edit *The Pedestal Magazine* (www.thepedestalmagazine.com).

FREDERICK BARTHELME directed the Center for Writers at The University of Southern Mississippi until 2010. He won an NEA Fellowship and numerous grants as editor of *Mississippi Review*, which he edited from 1977-2010, and online 1995-2010. He is author of *Moon Deluxe, Second Marriage, Tracer, Two Against One, Natural Selection, The Brothers, Painted Desert*, and *Bob the Gambler*, and a contributor to *The New Yorker, Esquire, GQ, Playboy,* and Epoch. His memoir, *Double Down: Reflections on Gambling and Loss,* was co-authored with his brother, Steven, and was a *New York Times* Notable Book of the Year. The same honor was awarded his retrospective collection of stories, *The Law of Averages*, published by Counterpoint. His novel *Elroy Nights*, October 2003, was a *New York Times* Notable Book of the Year and one of five finalists for the 2004 PEN/Faulkner Award. His latest novel, *Waveland*, was published by Doubleday, in 2010.

**KERA BOLONIK'S** essays, reviews, and features have appeared in *New York Magazine, Glamour, Bookforum, The Nation, Salon.com*, among other publications. She lives in Brooklyn, New York.

**JAMES BROWN** is the author of several novels, including *Lucky Town,* and the memoirs *This River* and *The Los Angeles Diaries.* His work has appeared in numerous publications including *GQ, The New York Times Magazine, The Los Angeles Times Magazine,* and *Ploughshares.* He teaches in the M.F.A. Program at Cal State San Bernardino.

**MARGARET BULLITT-JONAS** serves as Priest Associate of Grace Episcopal Church in Amherst, Massachusetts. A noted retreat leader and writer, she has focused recent retreats on divine/human intimacy, spiritual awakening, and the sacredness of Creation. Her memoir, *Holy Hunger: A Woman's Journey from Food Addiction to Spiritual Fulfillment* portrays her recovery from an eating disorder and growing up in a dysfunctional family. Her second book, *Christ's Passion, Our Passions* (Cowley, 2002) explores forgiveness, hope, and compassion in light of Jesus' last words from the cross. Her work has been published in a variety of journals and in anthologies of sermons, essays, and prayers. From 1992 until 2005, she was a Lecturer in Pastoral Theology at Episcopal Divinity School, in Cambridge, Massachusetts, where she taught courses on prayer, the spirituality of addiction, and environmental ministry. Margaret lives with her family in Northampton, Massachusetts. Her website is: www.holyhunger.org.

**MAUD CASEY** is the author of two novels, *The Shape of Things to Come* and *Genealogy,* and a collection of stories, *Drastic.* She has received international fellowships from the Fundacion Valparaiso, Hawthornden International Retreat for Writers, and the Château de Lavigny, and is the recipient of the 2008 Calvino Prize. She lives in Washington, D.C. and teaches in the MFA Creative Writing Program at the University of Maryland and the Warren Wilson low-residency MFA Program.

ANNA DAVID is the author of the novels *Party Girl* and *Bought* and the editor of the anthology *Reality Matters.* She's written for *The New York Times, The Los Angeles Times, Playboy, Redbook, Cosmopolitan, Details,* and *Vanity Fair,* among many other publications. She's the Executive Editor of *The Fix,* a website dedicated to addiction. Her memoir, *Falling for Me,* was published by HarperCollins October 2011.

DENISE DUHAMEL is the author, most recently, of *Ka-Ching!* (University of Pittsburgh Press, 2009), *Two and Two* (Pittsburgh, 2005), *Mille et un Sentiments* (Firewheel, 2005) and *Queen for a Day: Selected and New Poems* (Pittsburgh, 2001). A recipient of a National Endowment for the Arts fellowship, she is a professor at Florida International University in Miami.

B.H. FAIRCHILD has published several books of poetry and criticism, including *The Art of the Lathe,* finalist for the National Book Award and recipient of the William Carlos Williams and Kingsley Tufts Awards, and *Early Occult Memory Systems of the Lower Midwest,* which received the National Book Critics Circle Award in poetry and the Bobbitt Prize from the Library of Congress. His most recent book is *Usher,* chosen by *The Los Angeles Times* as one of their Favorite Books in poetry and fiction for 2009.

RUTH FOWLER grew up in the mountains of North Wales. She received a first class BA (Hons) MA MPhil in English Literature from Cambridge University, and then traveled the world eking out a living from writing, teaching, sailing, cooking and begging. Ruth lived in Nepal, India, Argentina, the South of France, the Alps, Florida, the Caribbean and

Central America before finding herself in New York, penniless and without a visa. This time in New York formed the subject for her first book, *Girl Undressed*, published by Viking Penguin (US) in 2008. Ruth lives between Los Angeles and London, and works as a journalist and screenwriter. She is currently writing her second book.

**DAVID HUDDLE** is currently Distinguished Visiting Professor of Creative Writing at Hollins University. He taught for thirty-eight years at the University of Vermont and continues to teach at the Bread Loaf School of English. Huddle's work has appeared in *TriQuarterly, The American Scholar, The Hudson Review, Story, Esquire, Harper's, The New Yorker, Poetry, Best American Short Stories, The New York Times Book Review, Shenandoah, The Kenyon Review,* and *The Georgia Review.* His novel, *The Story of a Million Years* (Houghton Mifflin, 1999) was named a Distinguished Book of the Year by *Esquire* and a Best Book of the Year by *The Los Angeles Times Book Review.* In 2012, LSU Press will publish his seventh poetry collection, *Black Snake at the Family Reunion,* and his third novel, *Nothing Can Make Me Do This,* was released in October 2011.

**PERIE LONGO** was Santa Barbara Poet Laureate from 2007-2009 and president of the National Association for Poetry Therapy 2005-2007. She has published three books of poetry: *Milking the Earth, The Privacy of Wind,* and *With Nothing behind but Sky: a journey through grief.* Her work has appeared in numerous journals and anthologies including *Atlanta Review, Connecticut Review, Nimrod, Paterson Literary Review,* and *Prairie Schooner.* She has been on the staff of the Santa Barbara Writer's Conference since 1984 and leads her own summer poetry workshop. As a psychotherapist, she integrates poetry for wellness, leading groups with Hospice and the Sanctuary Psychiatric Centers of Santa Barbara. She is poetry chair for the Nuclear Age

Peace Foundation and has been featured on the Charles Osgood radio show and in the *Huntington Post*.

GREGORY ORR is the author of ten collections of poetry, the most recent of which are two book-length lyric sequences, *How Beautiful the Beloved* and *Concerning the Book that is the Body of the Beloved*. He is also the author of a memoir, *The Blessing*; and *Poetry as Survival* about the survival function of lyric poetry. His recent essay about his work as a civil rights volunteer in the Deep South in 1965, "Return to Hayneville," was reprinted in three annual prose anthologies (*Best Essays 2009*, *Best Creative Non-Fiction 2009* and *The Pushcart Prizes*). He is a Professor of English at the University of Virginia, where he has taught since 1975 and was the founder and first director of its MFA Program in Writing.

VICTORIA PATTERSON is the author of the novel *This Vacant Paradise*, a *New York Times Book Review* Editors' Choice. *Drift*, her collection of interlinked short stories, was a finalist for the California Book Award and the 2009 Story Prize. *The San Francisco Chronicle* selected *Drift* as one of the best books of 2009. Her work has appeared in various publications and journals, including *The Los Angeles Times*, *Alaska Quarterly Review*, and the *Southern Review*. She lives with her family in Southern California and teaches through the UCLA Extension Writers' Program and as a Visiting Assistant Professor at University of California Riverside.

MOLLY PEACOCK is the author of *The Paper Garden: An Artist Begins Her Life's Work at 72* as well as six volumes of poetry, including *The Second Blush*. Her work is widely anthologized in *The Best of the Best American Poetry*, *The Best American Essays*, and *The Oxford Book of American Poetry*.

DIANA M. RAAB is a registered nurse and award-winning memoirist and poet. She blogs for the Huffington Post and teaches in UCLA Extension Writers' Program and in conferences around the country. She holds her MFA in Nonfiction from Spalding University. She compiled and edited, *Writers and Their Notebooks*, winner of a 2011 Eric Hoffer Award for academic presses, and finalist for Foreword Magazine's 2010 Book of the Year. She has two memoirs, *Healing With Words: A Writer's Cancer Journey* and *Regina's Closet: Finding My Grandmother's Secret Journal* and three poetry collections: *My Muse Undresses Me, Dear Anaïs: My Life in Poems for You,* and *The Guilt Gene.* She's the recipient of the Benjamin Franklin Book award for best health and wellness book for *Getting Pregnant and Staying Pregnant: Overcoming Infertility and High Risk Pregnancy.* Her website: is www.dianaraab.com.

SCOTT RUSSELL SANDERS is the author of twenty books of fiction and nonfiction including, most recently, *A Private History of Awe* and *A Conservationist Manifesto.* Among his honors are the Lannan Literary Award, the John Burroughs Essay Award, the Mark Twain Award, the Cecil Woods Award for Nonfiction, and fellowships from the Guggenheim Foundation and the National Endowment for the Arts. In 2010 he was named the National Winner of the Eugene and Marilyn Glick Indiana Authors Award. He is a Distinguished Professor Emeritus of English at Indiana University, where he taught from 1971 to 2009. He and his wife, Ruth, a biochemist, have reared two children in their hometown of Bloomington in the hardwood hill country of Indiana's White River Valley.

STEPHEN JAY SCHWARTZ is a *Los Angeles Times* Bestselling author who has spent a number of years as the Director of Development for Wolfgang Petersen where he worked with writers, producers and studio executives to develop screenplays for production. Among the film projects he helped develop are *Air Force One, Outbreak,* and *Bicentennial Man.* His two novels, *Boulevard* and *Beat,* follow the dysfunctional journey of LAPD robbery-homicide detective Hayden Glass as he fights crime and corruption while struggling with his own sex-addiction. Stephen has also written for the Discovery Channel and is currently writing his third novel, as well as a 3-D zombie film on assignment. He lives in Southern California and his website is www.stephenjayschwartz.com.

LINDA GRAY SEXTON is the daughter of the Pulitzer Prize-winning poet Anne Sexton and the author of the memoir *Searching for Mercy Street: My Journey Back To My Mother, Anne Sexton,* which was published to wide acclaim, optioned by Miramax films, and named a *New York Times* Notable Book of the Year. Her first novel, *Rituals,* came out in 1981; *Mirror Images, Points of Light,* and *Private Acts* were subsequently published over a ten year period. *Points of Light* was made into a Hallmark Hall of Fame Special for CBS television and was translated into thirteen languages. Sexton's most recent memoir, *Half in Love: Surviving the Legacy of Suicide,* is about her struggle with her own mental illness and the legacy of suicide left to her by her mother. She confronts deep-seated issues, outlives her mother and curbs the haunting cycle of suicide she once seemed destined to inherit. Sexton lives in California with her husband and her Dalmatian, Breeze. Her website is www.lindagraysexton.com.

SUE WILLIAM SILVERMAN's memoir *Love Sick: One Woman's Journey Through Sexual Addiction* is also a Lifetime television movie. Her first memoir, *Because I Remember Terror, Father, I Remember You,* won the Association of Writers and Writing Programs award in creative nonfiction, while her craft book, *Fearless Confessions: A Writer's Guide to Memoir,* was awarded Honorable Mention in *ForeWord Review's* book-of-the-year award in the category of "Writing." One of her essays appears in *The Touchstone Anthology of Contemporary Nonfiction;* others won contests with *Hotel Amerika, Mid-American Review,* and *Water~Stone Review.* As a professional speaker, Sue has appeared on The View, Anderson Cooper-360, and CNN-Headline News. Her poetry collection is *Hieroglyphics in Neon,* and she teaches in the MFA in Writing Program at the Vermont College of Fine Arts. Her website is www.suewilliamsilverman.com.

**JERRY STAHL** is the author of six books, including the memoir *Permanent Midnight* (made into a movie starring Ben Stiller), and the novels *Pain Killers, Perv,* and *I, Fatty.* Formerly the Culture Columnist for *Details,* he is a Pushcart Prize recipient, and his fiction and journalism have appeared in *The Believer, The New York Times, Playboy* and *LA Weekly,* among other places. His work has also been anthologized and widely translated, and he has worked extensively in film and television. Most recently, Stahl wrote the HBO film, *Hemingway & Gellhorn,* which premieres in 2012 with Clive Owen and Nicole Kidman. He is currently completing the screenplay for *The Thin Man,* starring Johnny Depp and working on a new novel.

**CHASE TWICHELL**'s most recent book is *Horses Where the Answers Should Have Been: New & Selected Poems* (Copper Canyon, 2010). She lives in the Adirondack mountains of upstate New York and Miami.

**RACHEL YODER** edits *Draft: the journal of process,* a publication which features stories, first drafts, and interviews with the author (draftjournal.com). She holds an MFA in fiction from the University of Arizona and an MFA in nonfiction writing from The University of Iowa, where she was an Iowa Arts Fellow. Her writing has appeared in *The New York Times, Sun Magazine, Missouri Review,* and *Kenyon Review,* among others, and has been selected for anthologies including *Best of the Web 2010* and *Rumpus Women.* Her website is www.racheljyoder.com.

# Index

# The Reflections of America Series

For more information and additional titles, visit:
**www.ModernHistoryPress.com**

CPSIA information can be obtained
at www.ICGtesting.com
Printed in the USA
BVHW071057100419
545158BV00003B/339/P